Understanding Difference

The meaning of ethnicity for young lives

Nicola Madge

Assisted by Steve Howell

NATIONAL
CHILDREN'S
BUREAU

The National Children's Bureau promotes the interests and well-being of all children and young people across every aspect of their lives. NCB advocates the participation of children and young people in all matters affecting them. NCB challenges disadvantage in childhood.

NCB achieves its mission by
- ensuring the views of children and young people are listened to and taken into account at all times
- playing an active role in policy development and advocacy
- undertaking high quality research and work from an evidence based perspective
- promoting multidisciplinary, cross-agency partnerships
- identifying, developing and promoting good practice
- disseminating information to professionals, policy makers, parents and children and young people

NCB has adopted and works within the UN Convention on the Rights of the Child.

Several Councils and Fora are based at NCB and contribute significantly to the breadth of its influence. It also works in partnership with Children in Scotland and Children in Wales and other voluntary organisations concerned for children and their families.

The views expressed in this book are those of the authors and not necessarily those of the National Children's Bureau.

Published by National Children's Bureau Enterprises Ltd, the trading company for the National Children's Bureau, Registered Charity number 258825, 8 Wakley Street, London EC1V 7QE. Tel: 020 7843 6000

National Children's Bureau, 2001
Published 2001

ISBN 1 900990 69 5

© British Library Cataloguing in Publication Data
A catalogue record for this book is available from the British Library

Designed by Jeff Teader
Typeset by LaserScript, Mitcham
Printed and bound by Page Bros, Norwich

Contents

Acknowledgements

Writing this book, and addressing questions that are at once important, complex and sensitive, has certainly been challenging. We are therefore particularly grateful to everyone who has read all or part of the manuscript and offered comments on both content or presentation. In particular we would like to thank Sheryl Burton, Predencia Gabbidon, David Gillborn, Shamsa Hersi, Melsa Houston, Nola Ishmael, Jane Lane, Mhemooda Malek, Shirla Philogène, Chris Power, John Rex, Philippa Russell, Ruth Sinclair, Mary Slevin, Letina Tsegay, Roger West and Derek Willis. Although we have listened carefully to all that has been said, we alone take responsibility for anything that we may still have got 'wrong'.

We would also like to extend our thanks to the young people from the Somali Youth Project and the Gheez Rite Eritrean Youth Project who talked frankly to us about their experiences as young refugees. Although it may be a tautology, we don't know anything unless we ask those who know.

1. Introduction

Children and young people in Britain come from a wide range of backgrounds and represent many ethnic groups of varying sizes. They have origins within this country and from around the world, have both black and white skins, belong to different faith groups, and speak a variety of languages. These young people live alongside one another and in many respects lead similar lives. For most, living in a diverse society is undoubtedly an enriching and positive experience. For some, however, it may signal difficulty and disadvantage. The purpose of this report is to bring together available information on the lives of young people in Britain, to examine what ethnicity means for them, and to identify some of the ways in which background contributes to different experiences and needs. Understanding such difference is a necessary first step in the celebration of diversity and the promotion of multiculturalism.

Ethnicity is something that we all have. In its widest sense it involves our culture, lifestyle, language and religion as well as our roots and origins. It can be a major factor in our self identity. It reflects what we think and how we feel, and hence our personal perceptions of ethnicity can vary with time, place and situation. How we are treated, and the status we have within the community, can also be affected.

In practice, however, ethnicity is usually described according to the broad classifications employed in official statistics, research studies and other documentation. This approach is far from perfect. These categories are not used consistently, and they cannot accurately reflect the young people who have more than one culture, lifestyle, language, religion and 'ethnic group'. Profiles of broad groups also obscure enormous differences between their members. The categorisation of ethnicity is, however, often the only practical possibility. It has, moreover, the merit of enabling those who stand out in their experience of inequality and disadvantage to be identified. Regardless of the individuals concerned, some groups may be disproportionately likely or unlikely to find themselves in particular life circumstances. It is important to know about such difference.

This report is reliant in the main on the definitions of ethnicity that have been used in the information sources consulted. It does, however, explore the meaning of ethnicity in its wider sense, particularly in relation to young people's personal identity. The two approaches need to be considered in parallel as a person's ethnicity category and their ethnicity as personally perceived are not necessarily the same.

The chapters that follow seek to understand ethnicity – in both these senses – and its meaning for children and young people. How different are the situations and experiences of young people from different backgrounds, and which differences matter? The aim is to describe not only the patterns of young lives, but also something about how these arise and develop. Are these patterns valued, are they necessary, what maintains them, and how might they be changed? By understanding more of the gestalt of young lives, and identifying the roots of inequity, pointers may emerge that signpost the way forward.

An enormous amount of material, which is highly variable in purpose, collection and presentation, exists on the issues and questions addressed by this report. The general remit has been to try to present a fair and evidence-based account with a prime focus on up-to-date publications and reports. Many life experiences are, however, very subjective and individual, and qualitative evidence has also been included to give greater insight into what young people themselves think – even though it is recognised that personal perspectives may well not reflect universal views. It is, nonetheless, important to listen to young voices if we seriously wish to understand difference and address unfairness and inequality in our society.

Many aspects of young lives are examined. First, after a brief discussion of definitions of ethnicity, Chapter 2 reviews studies on the development of ethnic identity and preferences and on young people's classifications of their own ethnicity. The evidence on differences in language, religion and other aspects of culture are outlined next, followed by a brief look at how these might affect the lives of young people who live 'between cultures'. Chapter 3 follows with a description of the size and geographical location of ethnic groups, and Chapter 4 continues by outlining differences in families and households according to background. Chapter 5 presents evidence on issues relating to income, housing, and residential neighbourhoods. Demand for, and use of, services during the early years are considered in Chapter 6, while those raised by pupils at school are the subject of Chapter 7. Educational attainment, school attendance, exclusions from school, teacher expectations, supplementary schools and multicultural education are among the topics covered. Chapter 8 considers differences in the years following the end of compulsory education, and the educational, training and job choices made at this time. Issues relating to health are considered in the next three chapters: Chapter 9 discusses physical health, Chapter 10 looks at disability and special needs, and Chapter 11 has a focus on mental health. Physical and sexual abuse is the subject of Chapter 12. Chapter 13 moves on to examine patterns of youth crime and youth justice, and Chapter 14 is concerned with the provision of social services. Chapter 15 puts the focus on the circumstances facing young refugees and asylum seekers in Britain across many of the areas considered in earlier chapters.

In order to set many of the previous findings in context, Chapter 16 looks at the community context in which young people grow up. Britain's history as a multicultural nation, the contemporary social context, and the legal framework are briefly examined alongside evidence on public opinion and the operation of the media. Chapter 17 focuses on children and young people and examines the meaning and manifestation of racism within their lives. Their reports of bullying and other forms of racist behaviour are outlined in this context. The issue of how racism might be addressed is also raised. Chapter 18 summarises the main messages of the report and makes a number of suggestions for the way forward.

While the main purpose of the report is to highlight evidence of difference, issues of policy and practice are also discussed and illustrated. A wide range of topics is considered, and it is inevitable that depth has been sacrificed for breadth. No claims are made for the comprehensiveness of the material included, and it is evident that many things have been left out. Nonetheless much ground is covered and it is hoped that a clearer picture of the meaning of ethnicity for young lives has emerged.

2. Ethnicity and Identity

Before turning to look at the available evidence on distinctions between young people from different backgrounds – evidence that is largely based on administrative classifications – this section considers ethnicity in its broader sense. It outlines some of the issues surrounding definition, briefly considers the evidence on how young children develop identity and preferences, examines the limited information on how young people describe themselves and their backgrounds, and highlights some of the linguistic, religious and cultural differences between ethnic groups.

Defining ethnicity

It is widely recognised that defining ethnicity is not always easy. Peach (1996) noted:

> While birthplace is an unambiguous category, ethnic identity is more mercurial. Critically, ethnicity is contextual rather than absolute. One may be Welsh in England, British in Germany, European in Thailand, White in Africa. A person may be Afro-Caribbean by descent but British by upbringing so that his or her census category might be either Black-Caribbean or Black-Other. Similarly, a person may be an East African Asian, an Indian, a Sikh or a Ramgarhia. Thus ethnicity is a situational rather than an independent category.

The changing and inconsistent way in which information on ethnicity has been collected at different dates is well illustrated by the variable Census definitions of race and ethnicity that preclude the direct comparison of demographic characteristics of minority ethnic groups over time. In 1951 and 1961 data on only country of birth were collected, in 1971 birthplace of parents was recorded (with ethnicity derived from indications of both parents born in a given country), and in 1981 there was no question at all on ethnicity (due to consumer resistance during the pilot stage). By 1991 a question on ethnicity was restored and gave respondents a choice of categories (White, Black-Caribbean, Black-African, Black-Other [please describe], Indian,

Pakistani, Bangladeshi, Chinese, Any other ethnic group [please describe]), in which to place themselves. For the Census 2001 this was changed again to make greater allowance for citizens with dual or mixed heritage. In England and Wales the following categories were used: White [British, Irish, Any other White background]; Mixed [White and Black Caribbean, White and Black African, White and Asian, Any other Mixed background]; Asian or Asian British [Indian, Pakistani, Bangladeshi, Any other Asian background]; Black or Black British [Caribbean, African, Any other Black background]; Chinese or Other ethnic group [Chinese, Any Other]. For 'other' and 'mixed' categories, respondents were given the opportunity to describe their ethnicity in their own words[1].

Amin and others (1997) pointed to the differences in language, religion, history and 'ancestry (real or imagined)' (Giddens, 1993) that contribute to definitions of ethnicity, and illustrated how this complexity was dealt with by referring to the 1991 Census:

> Respondents faced a choice between categories, some of which denoted national boundaries (Indian, Pakistani, Bangladeshi) whilst others focused on colour and/ or more general geographical distinctions (White, Black-Caribbean, Black-African). Such categories may capture the most crude distinctions that circulate in contemporary debates, but they exclude many ethnic groups and mask the wide range of variation between and within each named group. Most research uses some variation on the census categories and, in reviewing such work, we are forced to reproduce these distinctions. Nevertheless, it is necessary to remember that these groupings are complex, varied and changing.

The issues involved in developing suitable measures for recording diversity within the population were outlined in detail by Aspinall (2000).

While definitions of ethnicity are often intended as descriptors, they are sometimes employed for more political purposes. Richardson and Wood (1999) described use of the term 'Black':

> to refer to people targeted by racism, and to recall continually that race and racism are fundamental issues. To omit the word Black here (and to use, for example, a term such as 'ethnic minority' or 'minority ethnic' instead), would be to gloss over the realities of racism, and would in this way make the realities more difficult to address.

---

1 Slight modifications were made to the Census categories in Scotland to allow for Scottish, Asian Scottish, Black Scottish, and so on. In Northern Ireland respondents were given the options of White, Chinese, Irish Traveller, Indian, Pakistani, Bangladeshi, Black Caribbean, Black African, Black Other, Mixed ethnic group, and Any other ethnic group.

Similarly, Lane (1999) noted in a National Early Years Network report:

> The term **black** is used here in a political sense, to include all people who are likely to be discriminated against because of their skin colour . . . . The term **white** is also used here in its political sense. It includes all those people who are not usually discriminated against because of their skin colour.

However,

> the term 'black' . . . should **never** be imposed on a child, as some families may feel that this confuses a child's sense of identity. For example, some families from South Asia do not wish to be called black, and this should be respected.

Language and concepts, however, go in and out of vogue. The term 'race', for instance, is generally less used and less acceptable than in the past (Banton, 1987; 1988; Gillborn, 1990) even if, as Amin and others (1997) pointed out:

> Although 'race' is now redundant as a meaningful scientific category, the idea of 'race' (as a general descriptor of assumed national, cultural and/or physical differences) persists in society.

Despite all the discussion and the frequent and significant changes in the prevailing terminology, a lack of clarity often remains about exactly what is meant by terms used. These difficulties extend into the realm of needs assessment and service delivery. Richards and Ince (2000) observed how the Children Act 1989 refers to a child's 'religious persuasion, racial origin and cultural and linguistic background' but yet offers no guidance on what is meant by 'race' or 'culture'. There is also little indication, as discussed below, that the categories and classifications used bear much resemblance to those that young people would choose to describe themselves. The issue becomes even more complex as the population of young people from dual and mixed heritage backgrounds continues to increase, and as the vast majority of young people from black and minority ethnic backgrounds are now British. Increasingly terms such as Black British and British Asian are coming into common use.

Alibhai-Brown (1999) summed up these and other issues in her recent analysis of multiculturalism in contemporary Britain by saying:

> The terminology to describe diverse British populations is fraught with difficulties as terms are changing all the time to represent new realities. We have settled for ethnic communities, black and Asian Britons as our preferred terms. At certain key points we have been obliged to use ethnic minorities or ethnic minority communities or ethnic minority populations, but . . . these may not be suitable in the changing landscapes of the future.

The present report acknowledges all these difficulties and sensitivities surrounding the definition of ethnicity. For the purposes of the present review, it adopts a dual approach by which ethnicity is regarded in either a categorical sense or in terms of personal identity. The first, which follows the classifications used in the documents and reports consulted, is the only feasible possibility for examining much of the available evidence in the following chapters. It is, moreover, useful in highlighting differences between groups that exist over and above individual differences.

Understanding difference, however, depends on more than just comparing broad population groups. Young people's views about their own ethnicity and identity, and the role of language, religion, culture, customs and mores in their lives, are also highly significant. Evidence on these more personal and individual perspectives is outlined below.

The development of identity and preferences

Many writers have examined and discussed how children develop their own racial or ethnic identity, as well as the origin of their racial attitudes towards others (e.g. Milner, 1983). Early experimental studies in both Britain and the United States suggested that children became aware of ethnic differences at an early age (e.g. Pushkin and Veness, 1973). Studies with dolls indicated that most children could by three years say which doll was black and which was white, and that almost two in three four-year-olds and nine in ten five-year-olds could identify black and white people in pictures (Clark and Clark, 1947). Laishley (1971), in another British study, found that the majority of nursery-school children could distinguish between brown and white dolls, and that by four or five most knew which dolls had a similar skin colour to their own. Some studies have pointed to differences between children in these skills and suggested that white children may discriminate more accurately than black children. In Laishley's (1971) small London study, all six non-white children said they looked more like the white rather than the brown doll.

The interpretation of all these findings is, however, open to question. Studies in this area have often claimed to provide evidence of children's preferences, and commonly concluded that young children, both white and black, liked the white dolls better. In Britain, Pushkin (1967) and Milner (1970) found that both white and black children expressed white-skin preferences. Some studies, however, have suggested that the situation is more complex. Madge (1976) demonstrated that the skin-colour preferences indicated by black West Indian and white six- to seven-year-olds depended highly on context and the characteristics of the figures they were able to choose between. Adult approval was, for example, a more powerful influence on choice than skin colour. This tied in with American findings suggesting that young children's preferences for white dolls were linked to their awareness of racial discrimination and prejudice (e.g. Radke and others, 1949; Goodman, 1952). The overall conclusion is quite simply that attitudes to ethnicity are complex, even among young children, and reflect the fact that almost any real-life situation involves rather more than a simple choice based on skin colour.

Findings on children's preferences have led to concern about the meaning of ethnicity for self-esteem and ethnic identity. These are mixed in that some studies have found few differences between white indigenous and minority ethnic group children in these respects (Robinson, 2000) while others have indicated greater problems among the latter. Recently, concern has been heightened by the growing number of children with mixed-heritage backgrounds. It has been suggested that they may be at risk of both identity confusion and low self-esteem.

Katz (1996) examined theories suggesting that children from mixed-heritage backgrounds may suffer an identify crisis as they grow older. Some perspectives predicted difficulties for young people who grew up with white self-images but were treated as black, while others saw more problems for children who thought of themselves as 'mixed race' only to discover that society expected them to be either black or white. British evidence on this question does not, however, bear out these theories. Indeed as Katz (1996) pointed out:

> The only studies to report serious personality and identity problems in mixed-parentage children are clinical studies, that is, studies of children who come to notice because of their problems, as opposed to children found through schools or community networks.

Tizard and Phoenix (1993) carried out one of the main studies of children of mixed-heritage backgrounds. The young people in their sample came from predominantly middle-class backgrounds, and all had one white and one black African-Caribbean or African parent. Contrary to what some authors might have predicted, these young people did not display identity confusion because they were neither black nor white but tended to develop mixed-heritage identities. They seemed to know their own minds and the authors concluded:

> Most of the young people were clear that they made their own decisions about whether to accept or reject the constructions their parents, teachers and friends attempted to persuade them to use.

The findings from Wilson's (1987) study were similar.

A third investigation focused on families with a young child of mixed heritage (Katz, 1996). The main part of the study involved the close observation of two young children (7 months and 4 weeks at the beginning of the study) and their white mothers, but also included interviews with a small number of other parents. Katz hypothesised that racial identity and preference may begin to develop in the first year of life, but no conclusions would seem possible from the limited evidence he was able to present. He also reported that mothers thought their children needed to develop a positive mixed-heritage identity and developed strategies to help them do so. The strategies they used, he suggested, depended on both the mother's own upbringing and her social class, a factor that seemed stronger than race or culture in determining the family lifestyle. Again these conclusions need to be corroborated.

Most writers and researchers in this area have pointed to the positive aspects of mixed heritage. According to Yee and Au (1997):

> many children of mixed race grow up with a sense of belonging to both cultures and take pride in this dual membership

with problems mainly arising when parental marriages broke down. Moreover, as Katz (1996) pointed out, young people do not necessarily classify themselves in the same way in all contexts. A child with one black and one white parent may sometimes see himself or herself as white, sometimes as black, and sometimes as both. For parents, Katz reported that a lack of role models and stereotypes could be an advantage if it meant they could:

> negotiate culture and ethnicity within the family in a way that they could not have done with a member of their own group.

It is clear from existing studies that we have no clear and overall picture about how ethnic identity and ethnic preferences develop and are sustained. A better idea of the meaning of identity begins to emerge, however, as we consider the ways in which young people decide to describe themselves when given a choice.

Young people classifying themselves

An attitude survey among South Asian, African-Caribbean and white adults indicated that perceptions of culture and identity are:

> varied and complex. Most of the participants spoke of a mixed identity and did not want to pin themselves down to one cultural or ethnic category. A few even expressed suspicion and unease at the idea of being asked to categorise themselves in racial or ethnic terms. (Commission for Racial Equality, 1998b)

Furthermore, few respondents claimed to be 'English', a term which they seemed to find synonymous with 'white', although many seemed happy to be described as British.

Other interesting information on this question was reported from the Fourth National Survey of Ethnic Minorities (Modood and others, 1997)[2]. Respondents (who were classified as Caribbean, Indian, African Asian, Pakistani, Bangladeshi or Chinese) were asked during interview to 'suppose you were describing yourself on the phone to a new acquaintance of your own sex from a country you have never been to. Which of these would tell them something important about you?' They were then presented with 12 personal attributes to each of which they were asked to say 'yes' or 'no'. These attributes were: nationality, white/black/Asian, etc., country your family came from, religion, skin colour, age, job, education, height, colour of hair or eyes, level of income, and father's job. Patterns of responses were similar across groups for all items except skin colour and religion, with nationality, white/black/Asian, etc., and country of family origin, most likely to be mentioned in the hypothetical situation. Religion, however, showed marked differences according to background: this was mentioned by over two-thirds of the South Asians, fewer than half of the Caribbeans, and only one in four of the Chinese. By contrast more than six in ten Caribbeans, but around a third of the South Asians and only 15 per cent of the Chinese, said they would describe themselves in terms of their skin colour.

How do younger people regard their own ethnicity? There seems to be no simple answer to this question. Some evidence comes from a survey, linked to the European Commission's declaration of 1997 as European Year Against Racism, in which 505 young people aged from 14 to 25 years were asked in street interviews across the UK about their attitudes and opinions on Europe, Europeans and the European Union (Runnymede Trust and the Commission for Racial Equality, 1998). They were also asked about their own ethnicity. Although 14.1 per cent said they were black, 19.8 per cent said South Asian, 4.6 per cent said other, and 61.6 per cent white, most chose to qualify these descriptions. The vast majority, including three-quarters of the 194 young people from black or minority ethnic backgrounds, called themselves British. Of the rest, a notable proportion of black respondents identified themselves as English, and some South Asian respondents identified themselves as British Asian, British Indian, British Pakistani or Scottish Asian.

2 The series of four National Surveys of Ethnic Minorities carried out by the Policy Studies Institute (previously Political and Economic Planning) have yielded good information on minority groups within the geographical areas in which they are concentrated. The latest survey in 1994/5 added a large number of questions on culture and identity and explored health, racial violence and self-employment in considerable detail. As the surveys do not include many white people, and as they sample from a few areas, the findings cannot be used to produce population estimates. There was a 12-year gap between the third and fourth surveys, and the last survey is now several years old. As they are expensive and time-consuming to conduct, there are no plans at present for a further sweep.

It appeared that many of these young people identified themselves with both Britain and their country of origin. Fifty-five per cent of the black group said they were Black British while others said they were Black Caribbean (18 per cent), Black African (16 per cent) or Black Other (11 per cent). Half the South Asians described themselves as Asian British, and 31 per cent said Pakistani, 14 per cent Indian, 4 per cent Bangladeshi, and 1 per cent East African Asian. The report highlighted how the descriptors 'Black British' and 'Asian British' were more favoured by these young people than the standard census terms.

Interestingly, the vast majority of the young people in all groups did not seem to think of themselves as European and suggested that young people were not interested in Europe and nationality. The report concluded:

> It appears that young people are more likely to think of Britain as part of Europe geographically, rather than socially, culturally or economically.

Franklin and Madge (2000) also highlighted the mismatch that can occur between traditional classification systems and how young people perceive themselves. Their study suggested that many commonly used categories are very out of date and:

> may be largely dysfunctional from the perspective of young people whose ethnic and cultural identity has been shaped by a range of factors including history, geography and experiences.

These conclusions were drawn from a survey of over 2,500 7- to 16-year-olds who were asked to record their own ethnicity. The findings showed that how young people identify themselves is far from straightforward. At first sight it seemed that pupils fitted themselves fairly neatly into the CRE classification categories of White, Black Caribbean, Black African, Black Other, Indian, Pakistani, Bangladeshi, Irish, Chinese, and Other: some 47 per cent described themselves as White, 17 per cent as Black Caribbean, 9 per cent as Black African, 7 per cent as Black Other, 4 per cent as Irish, 3 per cent as Chinese, and smaller proportions as Indian, Pakistani or Bangladeshi. Nonetheless, the remaining 11 per cent classified themselves as Other and used a wide range of terms to describe themselves: more said they were 'mixed race' than anything else, some indicated a mixed heritage, and some just specified the country they identified most strongly with.

Interestingly, some pupils in the Other category described themselves in terms, such as black British or white/English, which might have placed them in one of the main categories if classified by an independent rater. The situation was, indeed, even more complex as a considerable number of pupils placed themselves in one of the main CRE categories but gave additional details incompatible with the main classification.

Pupils who indicated they were White, but who also said they were 'Black African, mixed race', provide an illustration. It was also apparent that there was no consistency in the way pupils of mixed black and white heritage viewed themselves: some described themselves as white while others said they were black.

Further evidence on the identity of young people from mixed heritage backgrounds comes from an interview study of 15- and 16-year-olds, three-quarters of whom were girls. Of the total sample of 242 young people, 58 had a black and a white parent, and the others had either two black or two white parents (Tizard and Phoenix, 1993). Less than half of the mixed-heritage sample thought of themselves as black, and the rest thought of themselves as brown, mixed or coloured, often saying they were 'mixed race' or 'half-caste'. Some, however, varied their self-descriptions according to the context, and 10 per cent of the mixed-parentage group said they sometimes thought of themselves as white. Sixty per cent of the sample appeared to have a positive racial identity, and nearly three-quarters of these thought of themselves as mixed rather than black.

Some young people illustrated how complex they found it to describe their ethnicity when they had parents from different backgrounds. According to one:

> I wouldn't call myself black. I mean, lots of people have said if you are mixed race you might just as well call yourself black, but I feel that is denying the fact that my mother is white, and I'm not going to do that.

Another had always called herself black, but was thinking about it:

> well I'm half black, but then I'm half white.

One girl asked:

> Do I have to choose?

The advantages of mixed parentage were pointed out by a number of children:

> Yes, I'm proud of my colour, you get the best of both worlds. You're not one colour, but two, and I think that's nice.

> It does mean that I'm comfortable with both white people and black people, which I know a lot of people aren't. And that also I'm accepted by both because I have a white family and a black family.

Tizard and Phoenix concluded that it was difficult to generalise about the mixed-heritage young people in their study who had little in common other than one black and one white parent and, for most, some experience of racism.

In another study, Wilson (1987) studied 51 six- to nine-year-olds with one white and one African or African-Caribbean parent and claimed to find little evidence of identity confusion. Wilson concluded that 14 per cent of the mixed-heritage children had a white identity, 8 per cent a black identity, 20 per cent were inconsistent, and 59 per cent saw themselves as neither black nor white, but as brown, 'coloured', 'half-and-half' or 'half-caste'. This 'intermediate' identification was made most often by children living in multiracial areas, whilst the children with inconsistent identities, or who saw themselves as white, were more likely to live in mainly white areas.

A report from ChildLine (1996) confirmed that mixed-heritage backgrounds are not described with any consistency. Callers to their service said they were mixed-race, 'half' an ethnic category or 'half' one and 'half' the other; or described how 'my Mum/Dad is black/Asian/Moroccan', or 'my mum is white and my dad is black', or 'I am coloured'. Some gave themselves pejorative identities like 'half-caste', and one girl introduced herself by saying 'I am what is called a paki'. Nonetheless, ChildLine concluded that almost all the callers in their study saw themselves as British, whatever their origin or birthplace, and however else they might also regard themselves.

> The picture here was of a group of clearly 'British' youngsters. If most children and adults have a sense of place as part of their identity, for these children, this country is their place.

Alibhai-Brown (2001) has described the 'complex lives of mixed-race Britons' and highlighted the implications for the personal identity of children who 'are not black, Asian or white'. Her view is that these young people may be rejected by all groups and have to develop their self-esteem in individual and unique ways. Much more understanding of the processes involved would be both interesting and valuable.

Language

Ethnicity includes language and the multi-ethnicity of Britain is reflected by its multilingual state. There are now 275 languages spoken by children in London (School of Oriental & African Studies, 1997) and it has been estimated that languages other than English are spoken regularly in up to one in three homes. The languages most commonly spoken by children in London are Bengali, Punjabi, Gujerati, Hindi, Urdu, Cantonese and Turkish as well as Mediterranean languages such as Greek, Spanish, Italian and Portuguese. Baker and Eversley (2000) presented further information on language among over 850,000 London pupils. They reported that, overall, 68 per cent spoke English as their main language at home, whereas 32 per cent spoke other languages.

Official statistics for England as a whole at January 2000 indicated that 8.7 per cent of pupils at maintained primary schools and 8.0 per cent at maintained secondary schools had English as an additional language (Department for Education and Employment, 2000g). Rates were, however, much higher in certain geographical locations. Over 43 per cent of pupils in inner London schools, and almost one in four in outer London schools, had English as an additional language. Within some inner-city areas, such as Tower Hamlets, Westminster, Brent, Newham and Hackney, the rate is nearer one in two.

Most children and young people, excluding recent refugees and asylum seekers, are nonetheless fluent or reasonably fluent in English. The Fourth National Survey of Ethnic Minorities (Modood and others, 1997) found that the majority of 16- to 24-year-olds from ethnic minority backgrounds are also competent in the English language. The lowest levels of proficiency emerged among females from Pakistani (84 per cent) and Bangladeshi (80 per cent) backgrounds.

Religion

Religion is another important component of ethnicity. Unfortunately the 1991 Census did not include a question on this and, until the findings of the 2001 Census become available, there is no detailed information on the size of faith communities in Britain. Estimates based on extrapolations from Census data on ethnic background, other sample studies, and information supplied by organisations within the religious communities themselves (Commission for Racial Equality, 1999) suggested that the most widespread religion was Christian (relevant to 40 million people) followed by Muslim (1-1.5 million), Hindu (400,000-555,000); Sikh (350,000-500,000), Jewish (300,000), Buddhist (130,000), Jain (25,000 to 30,000), Baha'i (6,000) and Zoroastrian (5,000 to 10,000).

These figures do, however, conceal the importance of religion and its influence on daily life. Although Britain remains a Christian country in terms of the relationship between the Church and the State, and Christianity is suggested as the dominant religion by the numbers given above, other religions may in some senses be more significant. The Fourth National Survey of Ethnic Minorities found that religion was, in general, most important for Asian groups and least important for white members of the population and the Chinese (Modood and others, 1997). The proportions from the different groups asserting that 'Religion is very important to how I live my life' were, in order: Bangladeshi (76 per cent), Pakistani (73 per cent), Indian (47 per cent), African-Asian (43 per cent), Caribbean (34 per cent), white (13 per cent), and Chinese (11 per cent). These findings were supported by the choices made by survey members when asked to describe themselves to somebody they did not know in a hypothetical situation (see page 10 above).

The significance of religion to the lives of people of Bangladeshi origin was highlighted by the findings of an attitude survey (Commission for Racial Equality, 1998b) indicating that religion was the most important aspect of identity among a group of 18- to 25-year-old Muslims in Glasgow. Some said they were 'Muslim, Pakistani and Scottish', for example, while others described themselves as:

> Bangladeshi Muslims ... Muslim first, obviously. That's the most important, that's what you are.

This significance may, however, be becoming less marked among younger age groups: 16-to-34-year-old members of the National Survey sample were, relative to older people, and whatever their ethnicity, less likely to feel that religion was very important in their lives. Within this age group religion was more important to those from Pakistani and Bangladeshi backgrounds (67 per cent) than to those who were white (5 per cent), Chinese (7 per cent), Black Caribbean (18 per cent), or Indian (35 per cent) (Modood and others, 1997). Qualitative accounts of religious beliefs and practices in Britain have been outlined by Lau (2000).

Religious practices vary enormously, even within broad ethnic groups. Sarwar (1994) discussed this in relation to British Muslim pupils who number half a million. Although sharing common beliefs, these young people have come from many different countries and have a variety of languages and cultures. Their precise needs are not the same even if they arise in similar contexts such as school assemblies, religious education, sex education, physical education, art, music, school uniform, provision for Muslim prayers, holidays and religious festivals, school meals, the curriculum, teachers and staff, and single-sex and co-educational schools. This is another instance in which it is clear that a young person's needs cannot be assessed by simple reference to his or her Census classification.

Culture

Culture is in essence an umbrella term for the aspects of ethnicity already discussed. It also describes a wide range of aspects of behaviour, attitudes and lifestyle. This section looks at just a few examples of where culture can mean difference.

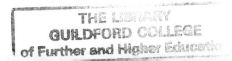

Asian young people may, for instance, be influenced by particular cultural expectations about dress and about male and female roles. Woods and Grugeon (1991) pointed to the difficulties facing Asian girls making the transition to secondary school where 'the prospect of showers after games lessons was alarming', as was the fact that 'There's a lot more man teachers', for many their first encounter with male teachers. Ghuman (1999) outlined a range of difficulties facing young Asians at school, and noted how teachers could also be caught in a dilemma between reinforcing their parental values or teaching them Western ideals of autonomy and personal choice. He quoted a teacher who said:

> Yes, girls have less freedom. The girls cope well in school and the majority accept that home is different. I took 9a to see King Lear. This father wouldn't let his daughter go, but I persuaded him. We are finding the parents approach us about their anxieties. When we assure them they [girls] would be safe, then they are more willing. But not on residential weekends; very few would be willing.

Cultural values can also influence the relationship between ethnicity and physical activity. Black parents have, for example, been reported to react negatively to teachers suggesting that their child is good at sport as they feel this downgrades the child's academic abilities (Sarup, 1986):

> One way in which schools are sponsoring black academic failure is through sport. There has been an upsurge of black involvement in sport at every level during the past decade in Britain. . . . It seems that sport provides the school with a convenient and legitimate side track for its disillusioned black low achievers and as a social-control mechanism. The over-representation of Afro-Caribbean pupils in school sports teams is in part the outcome of channelling by teachers who have a tendency to view this ethnic group in stereotypical terms, as having skills of the body rather than skills of the mind. By encouraging these allegedly 'motor-minded' pupils to concentrate on sport in school at some expense to their academic studies, teachers have re-inforced West Indian academic failure.

This view is perhaps exemplified by the following quotation from Sewell (1997):

> The armed forces tend to recruit people who are quite well-educated. One set of people are good at one thing but not so good at another. Your Afro-Caribbean is a big chap, often very athletic and more interested in sport and music. ('A Ministry of Defence spokesman')

Given the above, it is perhaps not surprising that there seems to be a perception that physical education is regarded as unimportant by families from some backgrounds. The view expressed by the then Health Education Authority (HEA, 1997) was that:

> Many parents of young people from black and minority ethnic groups consider sport a waste of time. ... Girls' opportunities are further restricted by parental concerns over their physical and moral safety.

Cultural background may also affect leisure patterns in other ways. Franklin and Madge (2000) found some differences in self-reported activities between 8- to 15-year-old pupils broadly classified as 'Black', 'Asian' or 'White'. Although numbers were small, members of the 'Asian' group were slightly more likely than the others to say that they did homework or read every evening at home. They were also by far the least likely to attend formally organised activities such as a youth club or Brownies/Guides, or to play a sport, on a regular basis.

A National Foundation for Educational Research survey (Harland and others, 1995) of 14 to 24-year-olds also found differences in how young people spent their leisure time. It seemed that members of the white group were more likely to go to pubs (18 per cent) than either Black Caribbeans or Asians (both 5 per cent or less), while twice as many Asians as black and white respondents mentioned watching TV and videos. Reading was most common among Asians (42 per cent) although they often referred to religious texts. Black Caribbeans (14 per cent) were the most likely to box or do martial arts. It is not clear how far these patterns reflect real preferences on the one hand and the availability of suitable and valued opportunities for leisure activities on the other.

Young people's attitudes and exposure to the arts were the focus of a survey carried out by Harland and Kinder (1999). This suggested that many poorer young people and those from minority ethnic groups were convinced that the arts were 'not for them'. These findings pointed to a role for schools in encouraging interest, and for theatres, galleries and other aspects of the arts in ascertaining that their programmes are attractive to all groups of young people.

 Some information on the lifestyle and culture of young people from black and minority ethnic group backgrounds is available from The Black Child Report 1999-2000 (Peoplescience Intelligence Unit, 2000). This presented survey information on 612 11- to 16-year-olds of African origin who lived in six areas of England with high proportions of minority ethnic groups. Young people were surveyed in main shopping and transportation areas and asked about their lifestyle in a range of areas: hobbies, watching TV, music, reading; health and fitness (ailments, exercise, sleep, self-perceptions of body weight, diet); smoking and drinking; religious activities and perceptions of self; education (including racism, exclusion, wish to attend an all-black school); and households and home life. Many of these areas related to important aspects of youth culture, such as musical preferences, dietary choices, doing things with families, but unfortunately the report gives little detail, provides no summaries, and does not undertake any direct comparisons either with the white population or between groups of black children. It is, nonetheless, a starting point for further inquiry into the broad cultural preferences and behaviour of young people today. Further investigation in this area would help to provide a better picture of the meaning of ethnicity for young lives.

Living 'between cultures'

Many children and young people growing up in Britain are influenced by more than one culture. This may be because they come from mixed-heritage backgrounds (see page 22) or because they encounter one (or more) culture at home and another or others at school and in the community (Community Relations Commission, 1976; Anwar, 1998; Bose, 2000).

Those encountering several cultures in their daily lives may adopt aspects of each. Modood and others (1997) found that almost half the South Asian young people in their sample felt both that they belonged to their own religious communities and that they were 'culturally' British. Dosanjh and Ghuman (1998) described such cross-fertilisation of cultures:

> This dynamic of enculturation ... can be summarised as comprising a continuity with some traditional norms alongside the adopting of some of the norms of British lifestyles.

While such enculturation can be a positive experience (Yee and Au, 1997), it may also signal difficulties. Bhatti (1999) illustrated how Asian children at primary school, especially boys, can feel alienated from the older generation. Having noted how:

> The limited amount of ethnographic research about Asian children at primary schools indicates the existence of potential mismatch between Asian children's homes and their schools' predominantly monocultural ethos.

Bhatti reported how his own ethnographic study had found that:

> Some boys felt alienated from the community elders and disillusioned especially with their so-called 'community leaders'. This disillusionment again was only expressed by the boys.

As one boy said:

> My father cannot understand me, how can he? He is so ... old fashioned.

Such findings further illustrate the richness and diversity of culture and its meaning, but also some of the dilemmas it can present for young lives.

Summary points

- Ethnicity is a complex concept that embodies aspects of skin colour, country of origin, nationality, culture, language, religion, customs and mores, and reflects a sense of personal identity.
- In practice, ethnicity is often discussed in relation to definitions based on classifications such as those used in the Census.
- Among the many limitations of defining the population according to broad ethnic groups is the problem of drawing generalisations that obscure the vast array of differences within these groups.
- Young people do not classify themselves in consistent ways, and very often use criteria incompatible with traditional classification systems. One implication of this finding is that commonly used ethnicity categories may be out of date.
- There are special issues for young people from mixed-heritage backgrounds as well as for those who experience cultural differences between home and community settings.

3. The Population in Question

What is the ethnicity of the British population and how are different groups distributed geographically? The best answers to these questions are derived from either Census[3] or Labour Force Survey[4] data. The advantage of the former is that the information covers the country as a whole and can be examined in relation to individual towns, cities and other specified geographical areas. Labour Force Survey data, while much more restricted in this sense, have the advantage of being collected on a quarterly basis and are accordingly more up-to-date and generally best for looking at likely patterns of population change.

The numbers involved

The balance between the majority and the minority ethnic population in Britain has changed significantly over the past decades. First, the number of people from black and minority ethnic groups has increased in recent years. It has been estimated that, between 1951 and 1991, those with roots in different backgrounds (but who may have been born in Britain) rose by a factor of around 28 (Peach, 1996) (see Table 3.1). Recent estimates indicate that the 2001 Census will show that members of minority ethnic communities comprise more than five million people, or one in ten of the total population. This compares with estimates from the 1991 Census that Britain's minority ethnic population accounted at that date for 7 per cent of the population.

---

3 The Census is a survey of the entire population of Britain, carried out on a set day once every 10 years. All members of households are asked questions on accommodation and relationships, demographics, cultural characteristics, health, qualifications, employment, workplace, journey to work and religion. The 2001 Census includes the most extensive information so far on ethnicity.

4 The Labour Force Survey is carried out in households across the UK. It began in 1973, was conducted every other year until 1983, and every year until 1991, and has been quarterly since spring 1992. Some 140,000 individuals, in 61,000 households, are covered and represent about 0.3 per cent of the total population. Each household remains in the survey for five successive sweeps. Weighted analyses lead to estimates of unemployment and other labour market indicators. The survey is likely to under-represent people living in London, in rented accommodation, young single people, and households with heads born in the New Commonwealth.

Table 3.1 Estimated size of minority ethnic groups in Great Britain, 1951 and 1991

Country of origin	Number in 1951	Number in 1991
West Indies or Caribbean	28,000	500,000
India	31,000	840,000
Pakistan	10,000	477,000
Bangladesh	2,000	163,000
Source: Peach, 1996		

Numbers of young people from Asian and black backgrounds have risen in line with these overall changes. By 1991, Census data suggested that non-white young people under 20 years comprised around 7.6 per cent of this age group in Britain (Warnes, 1996) (Table 3.2), and numbers are inevitably greater still some 10 years on. An increasing proportion of these young people has been born in the UK. In 1971, about 60 per cent of the black population as a whole was born abroad, with most of the remaining 40 per cent born to parents born abroad (Lomas, 1973). Now, a generation or so later, the vast majority of young people living in the UK were also born there. It has been estimated from Labour Force Survey data for 1997-8, that the proportions of under-16s born in the UK were: white, 98 per cent; black Caribbean, 94 per cent; black African, 61 per cent; other black groups, 97 per cent; Indian, 96 per cent; Pakistani, 93 per cent; Bangladeshi, 84 per cent; Chinese, 77 per cent; none of the above (includes mixed groups), 87 per cent; all ethnic groups, 97 per cent (quoted by Peoplescience Intelligence Unit, 2000).

Table 3.2 Ethnicity and young people under 20 years, 1991

Group	Number	Per cent
White	12,853,904	92.4
Indian	303,820	2.2
Pakistani	241,506	1.7
Bangladeshi	92,412	0.7
Chinese	47,448	0.3
Asian-other	58,941	0.4
Black-African	73,823	0.5
Black-Caribbean	134,745	1.0
Black-other	104,198	0.7
TOTAL	13,910,797	100.0
Source: (Warnes, 1996)		

Population projections suggest that the proportion of young people from minority ethnic backgrounds will continue to grow, with more than half the increase over the next two decades resulting from immigration rather than from births to mothers already resident in Britain (Office for National Statistics, 2000). This source, however, also predicted that the British population will continue to increase until 2036 because of inward immigration from a range of different countries: 'projections of 95,000 a year coming to live in the UK are based on the international passenger survey, asylum-seekers, those who enter as short-term visitors and stay for a year or longer and net migration with the Irish Republic'.

Recent years have also seen a change in the ethnic mix of the population as a whole as well as an increase in persons of mixed heritage. Between the summers of 1992 and 1998 it appears that the Caribbean population remained stable, the African population grew by about a quarter and the black-other population by about a half. The black mixed group also approximately doubled (Labour Force Survey quoted by Peoplescience Intelligence Unit, 2000).

The growing number of young people from mixed-heritage backgrounds reflects the increase in interracial cohabitations and marriages. Tizard and Phoenix (1993) noted how almost a third of those in their sample who were of West Indian origin, under 30 years and married or cohabiting, had a white partner. The Fourth National Survey of Ethnic Minorities (Modood and others, 1997) found that half of all black men and one third of black women born in Britain had a white partner, and about four in ten children under 16 and living with a black Caribbean mother or father had a white parent. By contrast, only about one in a hundred children from Pakistani or Bangladeshi families had a white parent. Better information on the mixed-heritage element of the population should be forthcoming from the 2001 Census.

Due to patterns of migration and settlement, as well as the relatively large families found among many minority ethnic groups, the age profiles of minority ethnic groups and the indigenous white population differ considerably. Whereas the white population has roughly equal age cohorts, each minority ethnic population has a younger profile, generally with a larger number of children and a smaller proportion of older people. In 1997, around 40 per cent of the minority ethnic groups were aged under 20 years compared with some 25 per cent of the white population (Office for National Statistics, 2000). This meant that while minority ethnic groups represented around 6.5 per cent of the overall population of Britain, they comprised 12 per cent of pupils in maintained primary schools and around 11 per cent of those at secondary level (Department for Education and Employment, 1999b). The largest groups of pupils are from Pakistani and Indian backgrounds.

Geographical location

The black and minority ethnic population is unevenly distributed across Britain, with higher representation in England than in Scotland or Wales. It is concentrated in large urban areas, and the two standard regions of the South East and the West Midlands account for 40 per cent of the total national population yet 70 per cent of the combined minority ethnic population (Peach, 1996). Within these regions there are further concentrations of minority ethnic groups within specific areas. According to the Department of the Environment, Transport and the Regions (1998) index of local deprivation, 56 per cent of people from minority ethnic communities live in the 44 most deprived local authorities in the country, and those 44 most deprived areas contain, proportionately, four times as many people from black and minority ethnic groups as other areas (Cabinet Office, 2000b).

Over half of Black Africans and more than 40 per cent of Bangladeshis live in inner London (Labour Force Survey, average spring 1997 to winter 97/98 GB). Dorsett (1998) concluded that:

> Overall, Bangladeshis live in the most deprived wards, followed by smaller proportions of Pakistanis and Black Caribbeans. Indians live in areas of higher deprivation than African Asians and Chinese. Whites in general live in wards with the lowest levels of deprivation.

At the time of the 1991 Census, the boroughs with the highest representations of minority ethnic groups were, in order, Brent (where minorities comprised 44.9 per cent of the population), Newham, Tower Hamlets, Hackney, Ealing, Lambeth and Haringey (Owen, 1992–95).

Recently available information on children in need confirms this picture. The new Personal Social Services Performance Assessment Framework Indicators (Home Office, 2001a) include a measure of the ratio of the proportion of children in the local population from minority ethnic groups. The first indicators for 1999-2000 demonstrated that, generally speaking, members of minority ethnic backgrounds were especially likely to live in deprived areas and in unpopular and overcrowded housing. They were also more likely than others to be poor and unemployed, regardless of their age, sex, qualifications and place of residence.

These patterns have implications for pupils at school. Bangladeshi pupils tend to be concentrated in inner London whereas black Caribbean and black African pupils are more evenly spread across both inner and outer London. In January 1999, Tower Hamlets (with 65.2 per cent of primary school pupils and 70.8 per cent of secondary school pupils from minority ethnic groups) and Brent (with 58.8 and 77.0 per cent correspondingly) had the highest proportions of pupils from minority ethnic groups (Department for Education and Employment, 1999b).

Despite the concentration of minority ethnic groups in certain conurbations, significant numbers do also live in rural areas. Isolation and racism can occur in these locations where issues of service provision and service delivery can present particular difficulties (Henderson and Kaur, 1999).

Summary points

- There has been a significant increase in recent years in the numbers of children and young people in Britain from black and minority ethnic groups.
- There has also been a notable rise in those from mixed-heritage backgrounds.
- The age profile of the minority ethnic population is younger than that of the white population.
- The black and minority ethnic population is unevenly distributed across the country as a whole, with concentrations in large urban areas, especially London.

4. Families and Households

The background of children influences the type of family and household they are likely to grow up in. This was demonstrated by a detailed examination of 68 families from three groups: African-Caribbean; Indian and African Asian; and Pakistani and Bangladeshi (Beishon and others, 1998). Striking differences were found in the frequency of multi-generational families, attitudes to married women in paid employment, the division of household chores, 'arranged' or 'negotiated' marriages, the value and significance of marriage, the acceptability of divorce, and approaches to parenting. It was notable that, whatever their individual views, most respondents, particularly the Asians, felt that they had little in common with white families.

Children and their parents

Marked contrasts by ethnicity are found in the proportion of children living with married parents, cohabiting parents or a lone parent. Table 4.1 presents relevant data from the 1991 Census.

Due to the effect of family size (see below), the proportion of lone-parent households is lower than the proportion of children who live in them. Census data for 1991 indicated that, overall, about one in five Black-Caribbean and Black-African, and one in four Black-other, households fell within this category compared with around one in twenty white households and only slightly more Indian, Pakistani and Bangladeshi households (Office for National Statistics, 1996). Table 4.1 also indicates that cohabitation was rare among Indian, Pakistani and Bangladeshi families. Overall, fewer than 2 per cent of households consisted of a cohabiting couple with dependent children. Rates of cohabitation were much the highest among Black-other and Black-Caribbean households.

These broad patterns were confirmed by the Fourth National Survey of Ethnic Minorities (Modood and others, 1997). This demonstrated how family patterns of

Table 4.1 Characteristics of households according to ethnicity, 1991

Children living in households headed by	married couple	cohabiting couple	lone mother	lone father
	percentages of ethnic group			
Black Caribbean	34	8	54	3
Black African	61	3	33	4
Other black	41	9	49	2
Indian	92	–	7	1
Pakistani	91	–	8	1
Bangladeshi	89	3	8	1
Chinese	88	–	11	1
Other Asian	88	1	30	2
Other ethnic minorities	63	6	16	1
White	78	6	16	1

Source: (Office for National Statistics, 1996)

both black and South Asian families diverged markedly from white families, although in opposite directions. Caribbean families were much the least likely to be found in long-term partnerships or to marry, and if they had married they were most likely to have separated or divorced without remarrying. At the other end of the spectrum, South Asian families were more likely to marry than white, and less likely to separate or divorce. One outcome of these patterns is that:

> The combination of the low rates of partnership, high rates of single parenthood, and high rates of mixed marriage means that only a quarter of 'Caribbean' children live with two black parents. (Berthoud, 2000)

Berthoud (2000) examined the issue of intergenerational links in more detail, focusing in particular on contacts between minority ethnic children and their grandparents. Based on data collected for the Fourth National Survey of Ethnic Minorities, he was able to address this question for the 1,390 minority group and 806 white parents for whom there were relevant data. Both similarities and differences between groups were found. Children of all groups appeared to be equally likely to have contact with their grandparents:

> There was no evidence that at the day to day level, any minority group placed more or less emphasis on vertical family links than white. Most parents regularly saw or spoke to their own parents, and grandchildren from every ethnic group had a high

chance of contact with their grandparents by that means if the latter were alive and in Britain.

Asian grandparents living in Britain were much more likely than those from Caribbean or white backgrounds to live in the same household as their grandchildren, and they were much more likely to live with their sons' than their daughters' families. Unexpectedly, however, there were considerable differences in the proportions of grandparents still alive in the different groups, which seemed to reflect the delayed age of parenthood among Asian, and especially Bangladeshi, men. Taking all factors including age and gender into account, there was a wide difference in the likelihood that children would be in contact with grandparents. At the extremes, 90 per cent of white pre-school children were in contact with their maternal grandmother while 3 per cent of Bangladeshi secondary-school children were in contact with their paternal grandfather.

Some authors have discussed the implications of close contacts with grandparents for childhood. Children growing up in extended families are more likely to have 'multiple attachments' to parental figures (Thomas, 1995) that may:

enable the small child to establish strong bonds with the extended family or clan which will be important for his or her future socialisation or welfare.

A Department of Health (2000a) report commented that:

For many black families living in England, wider family networks and connections are important not just to the individual family, but to the survival of the whole community.

Further information on this question would be valuable.

Family size

Based on the family size of respondents, the Fourth National Survey of Ethnic Minorities indicated clear differences in the number of children per family by ethnicity (Modood and others, 1997). Those from Bangladeshi and Pakistani backgrounds were particularly likely to have large families: 42 and 33 per cent respectively had four or more children as compared with 11, 7 and 4 per cent of Indian, Caribbean and white families. A further analysis of fertility within families, looking only at mothers aged between 35 and 39 years, showed that more than half the Pakistani and Bangladeshi families had four or more children as compared with fewer than one in ten of the white families. There seemed, however, to be evidence of a trend towards fewer children for women from these communities.

Marriage

Family patterns reflect the relative popularity of marriage among different ethnic groups. Census 1991 data showed that 61 per cent of white males aged 16 years or more were married compared with 42 per cent of the comparable Black population (Black-Caribbean, Black-African and Black-other groups combined), 69 per cent of the South Asian population (Indian, Pakistani and Bangladeshi groups), and 57 per cent of the Chinese and other groups (Owen, 1996). For the entire population the proportion was 61 per cent. A similar pattern was found for females of the same age. The proportion married was 56 per cent both overall and for the white population, but 37 per cent for the Black population, 69 per cent for the South Asian groups, and 57 per cent for the Chinese and other groups. Rates of widowhood and divorce were strikingly highest for the white population: 9.4 and 21.3 per cent of white males and females fell within these categories compared with 4.9 and 10.5 per cent of the combined ethnic minority groups.

Arranged marriages among Asian groups, although less common than in the past, still occur. Modood and others (1997) found that while only 15 per cent of 16- to 34-year-old African Asians and 27 per cent of Indians had arranged marriages, half the Bangladeshis in their sample and 65 per cent of the Pakistanis said their parents had chosen their husband or wife for them. Such marriages among Britain's Muslims may sometimes be between relatives. It has been reported that almost 80 per cent of arranged marriages within Birmingham's Pakistani community are cousin-to-cousin or uncle-to-niece (Haslam, 2001).

The trend is, however, away from arranged marriages. A survey of 107 Hindu and Sikh students, 70 per cent of whom were born in Britain, indicated that few were willing to follow in the footsteps of their parents (Francome, 1994). Nine out of ten reported that their parents had had an arranged marriage, and fewer than one in ten a 'love marriage', but 70 per cent wanted a love marriage themselves. This trend was supported by reanalysis of data from the Fourth National Survey of Ethnic Minorities (Berthoud, 2000), which indicated that most South Asians who came to Britain at or after the age of 25 years (and may already have been married) said that their parents had chosen their partner for them. However, fewer than half the Muslims and Sikhs, and very few Hindus, who were born in Britain or arrived before they were 10 responded in this way. There was no apparent difference between men and women in this respect.

In addition to those who have marriages arranged for them, there are other young people living in Britain who are forced into marriages by their families and communities. The Home Office (2000a) recently reported on a working group looking at this issue in which a forced marriage was defined as:

> A marriage conducted without the valid consent of both parties, where duress is a factor.

Case studies were provided to illustrate the problem which is known to affect people as young as 17 years. The report suggested that some young people stay on at school beyond the age at which they might leave simply to delay the time when they will be forced to marry. It concluded that greater awareness of individual rights, increasing dialogue between the generations, and clear and consistent messages about the unacceptability and consequences of such marriages, were among the measures necessary to curb this practice.

Teenage pregnancy

National birth statistics collected by the Office for National Statistics do not include details on ethnicity and so cannot provide information on maternal age according to background. Other data have, however, been used to derive estimates of differences between ethnic groups in this respect.

The Fourth National Survey of Ethnic Minorities in Britain (Modood and others, 1997) found that Black Caribbean women were most likely to have had children at 16-19 years (20 per cent) although less likely than Pakistani and Bangladeshi women to be mothers by 24 years (32 and 37 per cent respectively). Eighteen per cent of both white and Indian women were mothers by this latter age.

A more recent examination of teenage births and ethnicity drew on Labour Force Survey data for 13 consecutive years from 1987 to 1999 inclusive (Berthoud, 2001). Maternal age was calculated from the dates of birth of each woman and each child in the sample. This method, which is based on the assumption that most children continue to live with their natural mother until the age of 15 years, appeared to be robust. Broadly speaking, it was found that women of Bangladeshi origin (75 per thousand of this age group) were the most likely to become mothers before the age of 20 years, and those from Indian backgrounds (17 per thousand) were least likely. More women of Pakistani (41 per thousand) or Caribbean origin (44 per thousand) than white women (29 per thousand) became mothers at under 20 years.

It was not possible to determine whether women were married when they gave birth, but it was possible to record their marital status when interviewed seven years, on average, after their babies were born. Of the teenage mothers, 85 per cent of South Asians (Indians, Pakistanis and Bangladeshis) were married at the time of subsequent interview compared with 47 per cent of the white mothers and 15 per cent of those of Caribbean origin. Berthoud (2001) concluded that while rates of teenage births among white and Caribbean women had remained stable in recent years, rates for South Asian communities in Britain had shown a marked decline.

The Teenage Pregnancy Unit has, within its brief, to produce good-practice guidance for the 141 Local Teenage Pregnancy Coordinators that exist in every area of England on tailoring their services to the needs of local ethnic communities (Department of Health, 1999c). The progress report on the implementation of the Teenage Pregnancy Strategy (Department for Education and Employment, 2000b) also outlined how the Sexual Health Strategy has commissioned consultations with ethnic minority groups and that better data collection on ethnic variations will be a priority within the Teenage Pregnancy Unit's forthcoming research programme.

Summary points

- There are marked differences in rates of marriage, and the proportions of lone-parent households, between different ethnic groups.
- Family size and links with the extended family also differ according to background.
- The continued existence of forced marriages involving young people is a matter of serious concern.
- Age at motherhood varies between population groups.

5. Income and Housing

Evidence consistently shows how many black and minority ethnic group households, relative to the general population, are disadvantaged in both income and housing. These patterns have considerable implications for the children and young people growing up in such families.

Income and relative disadvantage

Income and ethnicity appear related within the population as a whole. Modood and others (1997) found that 41 per cent of African-Caribbean households, and 45, 82 and 84 per cent respectively of Indian, Pakistani and Bangladeshi households, had an income less than half the national average. The same was true of 28 per cent of white households. The large average size of Indian households meant that even where there was a relatively high household income, the average income per person tended to be relatively low.

The proportion of children living below various income thresholds has recently been analysed in more detail (Home Office, 2000b). Taking account of the ethnicity of the head of household (white, black, Indian, Pakistani/Bangladeshi, and other), and whether or not housing costs had been included, the numbers living in households with less than 50, 60 and 70 per cent of the median income, and less than 40, 50 and 60 per cent of mean income, were examined. Children living in families headed by a member of an minority ethnic group were more likely than those in white families to be below all the income thresholds. Fewer than 10 per cent of individuals in households with heads from black, Indian and Pakistani/Bangladeshi groups were, during 1997-8, in the top fifth of the income distribution compared with just over one in five in households where the head was white. This was particularly striking for children in Pakistani and Bangladeshi families. Comparable differences were found for 1997/8 to 1998/9 (Home Office, 2001a), and similar patterns emerge in many

Western countries where a disproportionate number of children from minority ethnic groups live in severe or chronic poverty (Spencer, 1996a).

Further evidence on relative disadvantage is provided by initial information from the new Performance Assessment Framework indicator on the ethnicity of children in need (Department of Health, 2000e). These data demonstrated that, despite much variation within and between different minority ethnic groups, these groups overall were much more likely than others to live in deprived areas and in unpopular and overcrowded housing. They were at greater risk of poverty and unemployment regardless of their age, sex, qualifications and place of residence. The data also suggested that children and young people from minority ethnic communities were disproportionately likely to be recorded as in need.

Housing conditions

Major inequalities in the housing market are not disputed. Black-Caribbean families are more likely than the population as a whole to live in local authority and housing association accommodation and less likely to be owner-occupiers. South Asian groups, except Bangladeshis, tend to have high rates of owner-occupation compared with the general population but often live in poor quality accommodation. These groups are also more likely to live in overcrowded conditions. Census 1991 data for Great Britain reported the following percentages of ethnic groups living at over 1.5 persons per room as: white, 0.4; all household heads, 0.5; household head born in Ireland, 0.9; Black-Caribbean, 1.3; Black-other, 1.9; other-other, 2.5; Indian, 2.7; other-Asian, 3.6; Black-African, 6.0; Pakistani, 7.9; Bangladeshi, 19.1 (Peach, 1996).

Many children and young people live in these households and share the housing conditions of their parents. There has been very little examination of the circumstances of children in their own right, although re-analysis of Census 1991 data has shown that black and Asian children were twice as likely as others to live in overcrowded conditions (Storkey, 1994).

Homelessness

Available evidence suggests that young people from black and minority ethnic groups are much more likely than their peers to become homeless. A study some years ago of around 2,000 homeless people in hostels and bed and breakfast hotels found that over one third of those under 25 years, and some 44 per cent of 16- to 17-year-olds, were from minority ethnic groups (Centre for Housing Policy, 1993).

More recent statistics from Centrepoint (2000) showed that 43 per cent of their client group were black and that 40 per cent of these were 16 or 17 years old. The report suggested that family breakdown was to blame for their homelessness and that 28 per cent of young black girls and 15 per cent of young black males said they had experienced violence at home. Nonetheless, it appeared that this group was less visible than young homeless white people as only 56 per cent, compared with 84 per cent of the young and white, had slept rough. It was suggested that this difference, which meant that black homeless young people may more often lose out on help and support, reflected the greater sense of vulnerability to attack and verbal abuse in this group.

The homeless day centre, The London Connection, has found that many young black people sleep on night buses or stay at all-night cafes, and then come to the centre when it opens in the morning in order to receive hot meals, friendship and safety, help with jobs and housing, and medical support.

> There has been a significant rise in the number of black kids who come to this centre; they now make up about 45 per cent of our total client group. Young black people face a number of issues and problems, not least that homelessness is viewed negatively by families and peers and tends to be far less visible. (Busari, 2000)

Renewing neighbourhoods

Poor housing tends to be found in poor neighbourhoods, and an important remit of the Social Exclusion Unit (SEU, 1998) has been to:

> develop integrated and sustainable approaches to the problems of the worst housing estates, including crime, drugs, unemployment, community breakdown, and bad schools etc.

as an English national strategy for neighbourhood renewal. The SEU (1998), which outlined the problems and their history, set out the first steps to be taken in tackling poor neighbourhoods as part of a complex multi-action process to be coordinated by the SEU. This identified some of the most deprived localities in the country, and noted:

> Taken as a whole, ethnic minority groups are more likely than the rest of the population to live in poor areas, be unemployed, have low incomes, live in poor housing, have poor health, and be the victims of crime.

The National Strategy for Neighbourhood Renewal was developed to meet this need and consists of a series of Policy Action Teams, No. 12 of which relates specifically to young people. Annex C to the Team's report (Cabinet Office, 2000b) described the particular problems faced by young people from minority ethnic groups and outlined how these need to be taken into account by the Policy Action Team (PAT) in developing a new approach to working with youth at risk. It stressed the need for proper information to identify differences by ethnicity and a proper evidence base at both national and local levels to monitor whether or not needs are subsequently met.

> At the caseworking level, the diversity of the local community needs to be reflected, either in the recruitment into mainstream services of staff who know how to work with particular communities, or in the franchising of services to appropriate voluntary and community organisations. ... One of the main reasons for systematically building consultation and involvement with young people into the way policies and services are delivered is to ensure that the aspirations and needs of ethnic minority groups are understood and acted on.

The Cabinet Office (2000a) outlined the work of the SEU and the PATs so far in relation to minority ethnic issues in social exclusion and neighbourhood renewal, and confirmed the disproportionate social exclusion experienced by many people from minority ethnic communities. The government has acknowledged the importance of including young people from minority ethnic groups in neighbourhood and community renewal in a range of initiatives to encourage employment, educational achievement, and to renew public services that tackle inequality. An example is the 79 new Millennium Volunteer (MV) projects for 16- to 24-year-olds 'to help tackle social exclusion in their area, improve their career prospects – and have a great time doing it' described in a press release as 'Thousands more opportunities to volunteer for young people from ethnic minority groups'. It remains to be seen what impact initiatives such as these will have within the community.

Summary points

- Children and young people from minority ethnic backgrounds are more likely than white young people to grow up in low-income households. This is especially true for those of Pakistani and Bangladeshi origin.
- These young people are also at greater risk of poor housing and homelessness.
- Neighbourhood renewal is a major strategy to try to tackle the problems found in deprived communities.

6. The Early Years

The early years are an important life stage when children develop attitudes and skills that lay the foundations for their later well-being, behaviour and achievements. There is, however, little comprehensive information on children's lifestyles and use of various forms of provision during this period. Those who do come into contact with services are in principle covered in many respects by legislation such as the Race Relations Act 1976 and the Children Act 1989 (Commission for Racial Equality, 1996) as well as subsequent amendments, although there is little monitoring in this area. Because of the significance of these formative years, it would seem to be a priority to gather much more systematic information on pre-school children to ensure that the needs of all groups, including those from black and minority ethnic backgrounds, are adequately met.

Demand for childcare

Before looking at patterns of childcare by ethnicity, it is worth considering whether there is anything to suggest that some groups might be more or less likely than others to require this type of provision. There is some indirect evidence on this question.

First, the employment rates for mothers of young children vary according to ethnicity. Mothers who do not go out to work may be at home and available to look after their children. They may, however, be involved in some other occupation outside the home and not in a position to be full-time carers. Furthermore, mothers who do stay at home may still choose to make alternative arrangements for the care of their children either within or outside the home.

Meltzer (1994) carried out a survey of a representative sample of households containing over 5,500 children aged under eight years to provide evidence on maternal employment and background. Of these children, around 89 per cent were described by their mothers as white or European, 6 per cent as Asian or oriental, and the rest as either West Indian or African, or other. It emerged that over half the mothers with white or European, and West Indian or African, children were employed, compared with one in three with Asian or oriental children and four in ten with children in the 'other' group. Mothers of white or European children were the most likely to be working part-time.

The Fourth National Survey of Ethnic Minorities (Modood and others, 1997) indicated similar patterns, although this also highlighted the enormous differences within broad categories, such as among South Asians. Thus while the main activity of 81 per cent of Bangladeshi women and 70 per cent of those from Pakistan was looking after the house and family, this was true of only 36 per cent of the Indian women and 26 per cent of African Asians. The comparable rates for white and Caribbean women were 27 and 13 per cent respectively. It was again found that white women in work were more likely to have part-time occupations than women from minority ethnic backgrounds.

Use of childcare provision may also be influenced by cultural differences in family preferences for how children spend their time before going to school. Income factors are also relevant in terms of a family's ability to pay for different types of early-years provision. It is evident that households with higher incomes are more likely to use more expensive forms of childcare.

More generally, take-up of childcare provision may be affected by factors similar to the take-up of many other kinds of services. These factors include: lack of knowledge of what is available or how to access it, a feeling that the services that exist are not appropriate, and the institutional racism inherent in some forms of provision (such as using waiting lists, which some families are more likely than others to get themselves on to, to allocate places (Commission for Racial Equality, 1996)). The use of other types of service, such as Family Centres (Butt and Box, 1998) is also relevant. Selective factors of these kinds are important in the British context where there are not enough childcare places to meet demand.

Use of childcare provision

Available information on the activities of young children during the pre-school years, when they may or may not be in some form of statutory, private, independent or voluntary, formal or informal, daycare or educational provision, indicates different levels of service take-up by minority ethnic and white groups.

The large-scale national survey of households with children aged under eight years (see above) carried out in 1990 for the Department of Health (Meltzer, 1994) reported information on how 3,243 pre-school children usually spent their day and who looked after them. Whether the child in question was White or European, Asian or oriental, West Indian or African, or 'other' (which, the report noted, mainly meant children of mixed-heritage described by their mothers as black British) was also recorded. The most common forms of day care, each used by just over one in five of the sample overall (some parents indicated that more than one option was applicable), were: no service received, the child was looked after by the father, or by a grandparent, attendance at a playgroup, or attendance at a parent and toddler group.

Some notable differences according to ethnicity emerged. Bearing in mind the unequal sizes of the different groups (almost nine in ten of the group were said to be white or European, over one in twenty were Asian or oriental, and around one in forty were both West Indian or African and other), it was striking that Asian or oriental children were almost twice as likely to receive no service as other groups. White or European children were most likely to be looked after by a grandparent, a nanny, mother's help or au pair, or to attend a parent and toddler group, and West Indian or African families were much more likely than other groups to rely on other relatives, day nurseries, or a registered childminder.

More recent evidence on the use of childcare emerges from a survey of parents with children aged 14 years or below in England and Wales (La Valle and others, 2000). Baseline data on the use of and demand for childcare in the previous week and in the past year were collected from over 5,000 respondents, and a more detailed survey was conducted among just over 2,000 of these to look at the factors influencing service use. Of parents in the main survey, 91 per cent were white, 3 per cent were black, 4 per cent were Asian, and 2 per cent (not included in the analysis) were from other groups. It emerged that minority ethnic parents were less likely than white parents to have used childcare, and this was particularly true for Asian parents. Childcare had been used in the last year by 88 per cent of white, 76 per cent of black and 56 per cent of Asian parents. The corresponding figures for the previous week were 59, 50 and 35 per cent respectively. Logistic regression suggested that ethnicity of a child was among the factors (although not the strongest) significantly associated with childcare provision.

The use of paid and free childcare was also examined, and ethnicity emerged as significant in this respect. Although numbers were small and necessitate caution in drawing any conclusions, it did seem that black parents were less likely to use childcare than white parents, but slightly more likely to pay for it (44 per cent compared with 40 per cent). A much more striking difference emerged for Asian parents of whom only 17 per cent said they had paid for childcare during the previous week. These findings are not, of course, restricted to the pre-school years.

Finally, the study suggested the possibility of higher levels of unmet need among minority ethnic than white families. Of those who had used day care, 41 per cent of black families and 19 per cent of Asian parents reported unmet need in the previous year. It was also found that only a third of black parents, but 43 per cent of white parents and 57 per cent of Asian parents, thought there was enough information on childcare provision. The Daycare Trust (2000) concluded from these findings that:

> Much more information is needed but it is clear that different black and minority ethnic communities have varying expectations of childcare services and demand for childcare.

The important role of the National Childcare Strategy (Department for Education and Employment, 1998) in addressing the needs of black and minority ethnic children and their families, and in meeting these needs, was stressed.

Early-years education

Two surveys have found that white children are slightly more likely than their counterparts from minority ethnic groups to be in early-years nursery education. As in the case of nursery provision, take-up depends on demand as well as availability.

The first of these studies looked at a representative sample of 7,000 parents of three- and four-year-old children and examined use of nursery education in both the last week and over the past year (Stratford and others, 1997). During the previous week, 90 per cent of white parents, but 85 per cent of black parents and 71 per cent of Asian parents, had used these early-years services. More striking, however, was the difference for three-year-olds: 81 per cent of those with white parents, but 57 per cent from minority ethnic groups as a whole, had attended nursery education in the past week. Differences were less marked for use of these services over the last year where the respective figures were 95 per cent of white parents, 90 per cent of black parents, and 87 per cent of Asians.

Prior and others (1999) reported a second survey of parents of three- and four-year-old children and their use of such services. Similar patterns were found, but the numbers in the minority ethnic groups were small. Children of white parents (94 per cent) were again slightly more likely than those from minority ethnic families (88 per cent) to have used nursery education.

Service initiatives

The National Childcare Strategy (Department for Education and Employment, 1998), mentioned above, is one of several initiatives covering the early years. Its purpose is to support families through providing good quality childcare appropriate to their needs, and the strategy includes the guarantee of a free education place to every four-year-old. Meeting the requirements of minority ethnic group families is specifically discussed.

The Early Years Development and Childcare Partnership Planning Guidance 2001-2002 (Department for Education and Employment, 2001a) on the provision of nursery education addressed equal opportunities within its Strategic Plan 2001-2004. Key goals were: to ensure all sectors of the community have equal access to childcare and early-years services, regardless of their gender, age, special educational needs, disability, background, religion, ethnicity or competence in spoken English; and to ensure that Partnerships have effective equal opportunity strategies which are monitored at least annually and that they ensure all settings identify and train someone to take responsibility for establishing and implementing the setting's equal opportunities strategy by 2004.

A series of guides to good practice for EYDC partnerships have been published. There is, for example, one on promoting play in out-of-school childcare (Department for Education and Employment, 2001b) that indicated how:

> Good play provision can be a valuable asset in promoting an understanding in children of the importance of their own and other people's cultures and ethnic backgrounds. Having a range of toys, books, pictures, games, activities, festivals and equipment from different cultures can help children learn about and understand the richness of the diversity in the world around them. However, this can only be truly effective in promoting anti-discriminatory behaviours if the attitudes of the adults who support children in their play have first addressed their own possible prejudices. Partnerships are addressing this primarily through training and support of childcare staff.

Organisations such as the Early Years Trainers Anti Racist Network (EYTARN) have also done much to address such issues among pre-school children, producing both texts (e.g. EYTARN, 1996; 1999) and videos (e.g. Benjamin, undated) to outline ways of promoting equality and dealing with racism in the early years.

Curriculum guidance for the foundation stage (Qualifications and Curriculum Authority, 2000) is also relevant. This stressed the need for a comprehensive rather than a disjointed approach to racial equality, and outlined aims and principles as well as features of good practice. It emphasised that practitioners need to be aware of the legal requirements of equal opportunities in meeting the needs of children from all social, cultural and religious backgrounds as well as for those for whom English is an additional language. The goal should be to provide a safe and supportive environment, free from harassment, in which the contribution of all children is valued, and where religious and racial stereotypes are challenged.

Sure Start (1999) is another important initiative in promoting equality of opportunity during the early years, and specific guidance on involving minority ethnic children and families has been provided. This outlined how:

> Services need to be designed to meet the particular needs of individual families, minority ethnic families, mixed race/heritage families, faith groups, and any other kind of family for whom the use of mainstream services may be problematic.

Some of the mechanisms for ensuring that these families have access to Sure Start and receive a high quality of service from it include accurate information on the local population, consulting with minority ethnic groups in the community, having an explicit objective about the needs of these groups, and providing evidence on how services meet their needs.

Similar considerations govern the provision of the new government-funded Children's Fund services. All these should have:

> a strategy for reaching black and ethnic minority users, travellers, disabled people and other hard-to-reach groups irrespective of their numbers in the population. (Children and Young People's Unit, 2001)

Staff and volunteers should accordingly be able to work effectively in multicultural communities, or undertake training on the 'benefits of ethnic diversity' if working in a predominantly white area. A golden rule for services is, moreover, that they should be flexible enough to respond to individual needs but yet joined-up enough to be able to address all relevant concerns.

Monitoring by ethnicity

Although there is currently very little monitoring by ethnicity in relation to the early years, guidance on structures and procedures may lead to greater practice in this area in the next few years. Much of the information available at present comes from individual surveys where the numbers of children from minority ethnic backgrounds can be small and where children from broad ethnic groups are classified together and obscure the differences between the component groups.

Summary points

- Mothers of pre-school children show different patterns of employment according to ethnicity. These may affect the demand for early-years provision within different groups.
- Varying levels of take-up of pre-school childcare services are found across ethnic groups.
- Government-funded early-years initiatives, such as the Early Years Development and Childcare Partnerships, stress the need to promote an understanding of diversity among pre-school children.
- These partnerships, as well as other initiatives such as Sure Start and the Children's Fund services, emphasise the importance of targeting black and minority ethnic users.

7. Pupils at School

Around one in eight children and young people in Britain is from a black or minority ethnic background and the vast majority are at school. As already described, these pupils tend to be concentrated in certain geographical locations, notably London and other large conurbations. In many London schools there are, accordingly, more pupils from non-white than from white backgrounds. Most of these young people are fluent in English although many also speak another language at home.

Issues surrounding schooling and ethnicity cause considerable concern. Patterns of attainment and achievement vary according to background, and variable rates of school exclusion are also often found. It is widely held that some teachers hold different attitudes towards, and expectations of, young people from black and minority ethnic groups, and there is some evidence of institutional racism within schools. Supplementary schools have grown in number to meet the special needs of many minority ethnic groups, and a wide range of programmes and initiatives have been developed to promote multicultural education and to encourage equal opportunities for all.

Educational attainment

Although there has never been any national monitoring of pupil performance by ethnicity, sample studies over several decades have consistently found differences in educational attainment according to background. Early studies (e.g. Little and others, 1968; Payne, 1969; Yule and others, 1975) indicated that differences were found between minority ethnic and white pupils whatever the country of origin of the parents. Even where black and minority ethnic group children had high IQ levels, reading attainment was often still below age level (Bagley, 1971). The Black Peoples Progressive Association and Redbridge Community Relations Council (1978), in another important early report into the underachievement of West Indian pupils in Redbridge, demonstrated that low performance was not just an inner city phenomenon but also occurred among pupils living in reasonably comfortable conditions. Other seminal papers on this issue, based on a series of studies carried out by the Inner London Education Authority (1969; 1973; 1983a and b), confirmed these general findings.

Continuing interest in this issue in recent years was marked by the publication of the Swann Report (1985), which reported on the findings of the Committee of Inquiry into the Education of Children from Ethnic Minority Groups. This far-reaching inquiry drew the following conclusion:

> West Indian children, on average, are underachieving at school. Asian children, by contrast, show on average, a pattern of achievement which resembles that of White children, though there is some evidence of variation between different sub-groups. Bangladeshis in particular are seriously underachieving. Such evidence as there is suggests that of the smaller ethnic minorities, some are underachieving and some are not. Averages, of course, conceal much variation; there are West Indian children who do well, as well as Asian children who are underachieving.

Gillborn and Gipps (1996) resurrected the debate and pointed to the lack of good data on which to assess the attainment of pupils from different backgrounds. They showed how in Birmingham, where there are the highest concentrations of pupils from minority ethnic backgrounds, the gap between the African-Caribbean (the lowest achieving group) and the white pupils (the highest achieving group) increased so that whereas one in three of the latter group gained this standard, only one in seven of the African-Caribbean pupils did so (Gillborn and Gipps, 1996). An increased gap between the performance of the South Asian and the African-Caribbean pupils in Brent was also reported. Nonetheless in Tower Hamlets, where almost one in four Bangladeshi children of compulsory school age live, more Bangladeshi than white pupils reached this standard.

A subsequent report from Ofsted (1999) looked at attainment by ethnicity in a national sample of 48 schools (half primary and half secondary) in 25 local education authorities. These schools do not provide a fully representative sample, but were selected according to the proportion of pupils from each of four minority groups: Bangladeshi, Black Caribbean, Pakistani and gypsy traveller. Black Caribbean pupils appeared to be achieving at national average level in primary schools but underachieving at secondary level, Pakistani pupils performed poorly at primary and secondary schools but often 'caught up' with other groups at GCSE level in schools where achievement tended to be below the national average, and Bangladeshi pupils generally performed below the national average although they were:

a group making slow but steady progress and reaching a level that compares favourably with other pupils in socio-economically disadvantaged schools by time of GCSE.

Probably the best data on performance at secondary level are provided by the Youth Cohort Study[5], even though these are based on a small sample and a low representation of pupils from minority ethnic backgrounds. Findings over the first ten year period (1988 to 1997) were examined in detail by Gillborn and Mirza (2000). Based on an analysis of those in state schools only, they found that by 1997 the highest level of attainment was shown by the Indian group, 49 per cent of whom gained at least five GCSE passes at A* to C level. Next was the white group (44 per cent), followed by Bangladeshis (32 per cent), and then those from black and Pakistani groups (28 per cent in each case). Looking at patterns of attainment over the full ten-year period, it emerged that all groups had made gains but that these had not been equal. The greatest gains were made by the Indian pupils, who overtook their white peers, and the least by the Pakistani and black groups. The gap between pupils from African-Caribbean and Pakistani backgrounds and from white backgrounds was greater than ten years previously. These findings appeared to be largely independent of social class. African-Caribbean pupils from non-manual homes had a lower attainment level than other pupils from similar backgrounds and indeed their achievement was often comparable to that shown by other minority ethnic group pupils from manual backgrounds. Girls tended to attain at a higher level than boys in each ethnic group.

The most recent sweep of the Youth Cohort Study (Department for Education and Employment, 2001d) included information on attainment patterns in 1999 for all pupils (i.e. not only those in state schools). This demonstrated that achievement levels increased over a two-year period for all groups except those of Bangladeshi origin. By this later date 70 per cent of other Asian groups, 62 per cent of those classified as Indian, 50 per cent of the white pupils, 37 per cent of the black group, and 30 per cent of both the Bangladeshi and Pakistani groups, achieved at least five GCSE higher-level passes. These changes suggested that the gap between the highest and lowest achievers had widened over the two years.

---

5 The Youth Cohort Study is a series of longitudinal studies of cohorts of 16-year-olds who are also followed up one and/or two years later. There have been ten sweeps of this study, the last in 2000 with a 55 per cent response rate from a cohort of 25,000 young people. Data are collected in the spring on the GCSE results the previous summer, and a weighted analysis examines the proportion of pupils in each minority ethnic group to have gained five or more passes at A* to C grades. Limitations of the YCS are the small sample sizes, the particularly high non-response rates for black groups, and problems of continuing responses from survey members.

Gillborn and Mirza (2000) also examined data collected from 118 unnamed local education authorities applying for the Ethnic Minority Achievement Grant (EMAG). Based on the two in three who were able to provide information on attainment by ethnicity, it appeared that while white pupils usually attained at higher levels than black pupils, Indian pupils were outperforming their white peers in 8 out of 10 authorities. There was, however, considerable variability between authorities with each minority ethnic group achieving higher than all others in at least one region. Indeed in about one in four authorities, the Bangladeshi group was performing at a higher level than white pupils. Although these findings were based on a non-representative selection of authorities, they do indicate the significance that local context and school intake can have on patterns of attainment.

Another important finding from this study concerned the educational careers of pupils from different backgrounds. Six of the authorities included baseline data in their EMAG submissions and were able to examine longitudinal progress according to ethnicity. In one large urban authority it emerged that whereas African-Caribbean pupils had entered the educational system as the highest-achieving group, they had left with the smallest proportion gaining five higher-grade GCSEs. Furthermore, the relative attainment of this group declined at each Key Stage. Although it is unclear how far these findings are generalisable, they are striking in showing what can happen. As Gillborn and Mirza (2000) concluded:

> That any ethnic group could enter school 20 percentage points in advance of the average but leave 21 points behind, opens up an important area for educational debate on ethnic minority attainment.

The overall picture is indeed far from straightforward. Another published study on attainment by ethnicity during the early years, which examined verbal and non-verbal cognitive skills upon entry to pre-school education (Sammons and others, 1999), found that highest scores were achieved by white children and lowest scores by Pakistani and then black African children. These findings should, however, be regarded with caution as they refer to only a very small sample of children and as some of the differences between the groups may have been attributable to background differences such as parental educational and occupational levels.

Strand (1999) examined the educational progress of some 5,000 pupils, comprising three cohorts from consecutive years, attending 55 primary schools in an inner-London local education authority. Ethnicity, sex and entitlement to free school meals were all found individually, and in interaction, to relate to progress between the baseline assessment at four years and the tests at the end of Key Stage 1 at age seven. In general, pupils from white backgrounds made more progress than those from the

Caribbean, but less than Chinese pupils. Least progress overall was made by Caribbean and 'black other' boys, African and Caribbean pupils who had achieved high baseline scores, and English, Scottish, Welsh and Northern Irish pupils entitled to free school meals.

It is apparent that a range of factors influence attainment, and that ethnicity is but one of these. There is, for example, likely to be a complex association between gender, socio-economic status, ethnic group and educational achievement. Gillborn and Mirza (2000) concluded, nonetheless, that although social class and gender are associated with differences in attainment, these factors alone are not sufficient to account for the inequalities between ethnic groups.

School attendance

There are no national or large-scale survey data on school attendance by ethnicity, and the only available statistics of education in this area examine school rates against school composition. Looking at both authorised and unauthorised absence from school, these have shown that rates of both go up as the proportion of pupils known to be eligible for free school meals increases and, in general, as schools have greater proportions of pupils from each minority ethnic group except for the Chinese. Comparing schools with the lowest (up to 0.1 per cent) and highest (2 per cent or more) rates of unauthorised absences during 1999/2000, minority ethnic group pupils represented 2.7 and 12.5 per cent of the school population respectively. Proportionately, the changing representation of pupils of Bangladeshi origin was particularly striking (Department for Education and Employment, 2000f). These findings are perhaps unsurprising. Schools with high rates of eligibility for free school meals, and those with a high proportion of minority ethnic pupils, are both likely to reflect an intake with a relatively high degree of socio-economic disadvantage.

Exclusions from school

The disproportionate numbers of pupils from black and minority ethnic backgrounds excluded from school have been repeatedly reported in recent years. Gillborn (1996) indicated how permanent exclusions had risen across all ethnic groups over the previous few years, and how those most likely to be excluded were pupils from African-Caribbean and mixed-heritage backgrounds. Much the same pattern has continued to occur.

Recent statistics on permanent exclusions provided by the Schools Census[6] for 1998/9 illustrate the numbers currently involved (Department for Education and Employment, 2000c). These show, first, that the vast majority of excluded pupils are white, but second that the likelihood of exclusion is influenced by ethnicity. Overall, 84.5 per cent of excluded pupils were white, while 5.5 per cent were black Caribbean, 1.5 per cent black African, and 2.6 per cent black Other. Pupils from Indian, Pakistani and Bangladeshi backgrounds accounted for 2.7 per cent of all exclusions. Risk of exclusion was, however, very different. On this measure, black pupils (0.58, 0.21 and 0.49 per cent of their ethnic group respectively for black Caribbean, black African and black other pupils) were much more likely to be excluded than white pupils (0.15 per cent) who were, in turn, more at risk than pupils from East Asian backgrounds (0.04, 0.10 and 0.07 per cent of Indian, Pakistani and Bangladeshi pupils).

These figures, nonetheless, represented a slight reduction in exclusions for all groups compared to the previous year. It was suggested that the gap between groups may also be narrowing as exclusions fell by 15 per cent overall but by 19 per cent among black pupils. A contrary trend was, however, indicated by Kinder and others (2000): a survey of 30 LEAs suggested that rates of excluded Bangladeshi boys and African-Caribbean girls were in fact rising, and also demonstrated that some groups with above-average exclusion rates (e.g. Croatians) were not represented in the statistics.

A number of intervention measures have been introduced to reduce exclusions. Pupil Referral Units have existed in a growing number of authorities since 1997 to provide education for excluded pupils, and by 2001 there were over a thousand Learning Support Units (with a capacity to work with at least 10,000 pupils at a time) within schools to support disruptive pupils. Official statistics indicating reductions in exclusions have led to claims that these intervention measures have begun to have an impact. Nonetheless, the reduction in numbers has not been even across groups and representation among some groups may well have increased. It is certainly too early to be able to give a clear verdict on the impact these initiatives may have had.

---

6 The Department for Education and Employment Schools Census has been based since 1945/6 on a series of returns from schools providing details of pupils, staff, classes and examination courses on a date in January. It provides a snapshot picture, although sometimes retrospective data are also collected (e.g. number of permanent exclusions during the previous year). It includes returns from primary, middle and secondary schools, and has a response rate of about 95 per cent. About 26,300 schools in England received forms as part of the census in 1998. Information on the ethnic composition of pupils, the number of pupils with English as an additional language, and the number of exclusions according to ethnic group are published in Department for Education and Employment Statistical Press Notices and Statistical Bulletins.

Teacher expectations and educational practice

Although difficult to demonstrate empirically, a number of reports have presented qualitative evidence to suggest that teachers may treat pupils in different ways according to their ethnic background. It has also been suggested that teacher expectations about pupils' attainment levels are given institutional backing and so become more likely to be fulfilled.

Apart from one noteable exception (Foster, 1990), the vast majority of studies carried out in multi-ethnic schools have concluded that, consciously or unconsciously, teachers can act in ways that disadvantage pupils from minority ethnic backgrounds. Sometimes it has been observed that African-Caribbean pupils, especially boys, receive more severe criticism than others involved in similar misbehaviour. Gillborn (1990) suggested that conflictual relationships arose between teachers and African-Caribbean pupils not because they were challenging authority but because they experienced school differently and behaved accordingly. Teachers did not have the same expectations of them as they had of South Asian pupils who acted much more like the white pupils. He argued that although the teachers' actions were not overtly racist, their consequences clearly disadvantaged black pupils. Other authors have high-lighted the way in which stereotypes can be perpetuated:

> There may be no conscious attempt to treat black youth in a different way to white youth, but the unintended teacher effects result in differential responses, which work against black youth .... There was a tendency for Asian male students to be seen by the teachers as technically of 'high ability' and socially as conformist. Afro-Caribbean male students tended to be seen as having 'low ability' and potential discipline problems. (Mac an Ghaill, 1988)

Gillborn and Gipps (1996) reported:

> Some qualitative research suggests there are relatively high levels of tension between white teachers and black pupils, with teachers complaining about 'troublesome' black pupils and disproportionately criticising them, and black pupils responding to expectations of low ability and disruptive behaviour.

A similar conclusion was reached by Amin and others (1997) who reviewed qualitative research in this area and pointed to the contrasting situations of pupils from African-Caribbean and South Asian backgrounds. Findings suggested that 'high degrees of control and criticism' at all levels of schooling characterise the relationships between African-Caribbean pupils and their white teachers. The teachers, even if committed to equality of opportunity, see their behaviour as disruptive and a challenge to their authority and are, for this reason, more likely to place them in low-status teaching groups. By contrast:

> Teachers often hold negative and patronising stereotypes about South Asian students ... [and] ... Problems with language can sometimes be misinterpreted as signifying a deeper seated learning problem, leading to South Asian students sometimes being placed in teaching groups of a lower standing than their abilities might warrant.

More recently, an Ofsted (2001) report on secondary school inspections provided evidence of how teacher attitudes and behaviour may affect exclusion rates. This suggested that boys from Black Caribbean and mixed heritage backgrounds were more likely than others to be excluded for 'challenging behaviour' whereas white pupils were particularly likely to be excluded for swearing. Skin colour did not seem to distinguish between those disciplined for violence. Where behaviour was similar, it appeared that black pupils were often excluded for longer periods. Also, teachers sometimes seemed reluctant to discipline black pupils for lesser offences in case they were accused of racism. An escalation in antisocial behaviour, and consequent exclusion, was one outcome. The report observed how many black pupils felt they were treated unfairly because of their ethnicity, and called for much more open debate in schools about the issues involved. A range of other studies have corroborated these general conclusions (Connolly, 1998; Sewell, 1997; Wright, 1986; 1992; Wright and others, 2000) and indicated that further examination of these questions is warranted.

Qualitatively, there is also evidence that black young people can feel that teachers have low expectations of them and treat them accordingly, and it appears that optimal relations between pupils and teachers may depend upon changes on both sides. According to Gillborn (1990):

> If able black pupils are to succeed they need not only to be prepared to work hard but they must also behave in a way which does not reinforce the perception that they are a threat to the teacher's authority.

In order to investigate the role of some of the school processes reinforcing teacher expectations of pupil attainment, Gillborn and Youdell (2000) conducted a study of two secondary schools in multi-ethnic areas of London. Major educational reforms over recent years have increased the pressure on schools to raise standards, and it seemed that a range of practices had developed which on the one hand helped schools achieve the goals laid down by government but on the other discriminated against the pupils who were already at greatest disadvantage. Practices such as GCSE tiering (whereby pupils are entered for examinations at different levels and can be restricted to achieving only lower grades) and setting, were in particular giving institutional force to teacher expectations of pupil attainment. The research suggested that:

> teacher racism is not as simple and crude as some commentators might anticipate. Openly racist teachers and consciously discriminating practices are rare. Yet widespread inequalities of opportunity are endured by Black children, seen in national achievement statistics and echoed in our case-study schools.

Teachers and teacher training

A number of reports have discussed the role of teachers and the training they require to meet the needs of pupils from diverse backgrounds. The Teacher Training Agency has pointed to the lack of minority ethnic teachers and headteachers (TTA, 1999). Earley and others (1999) have also noted the underrepresentation of school governors from these backgrounds, and suggested that the proportion of black and Asian trainee teachers should be increased from 7 to 9 per cent by 2005 (TTA, 2000). The National Union of Schoolmasters/Union of Women Teachers (1999) also highlighted the ethnic composition of teachers and indicated the under-representation of ethnic minorities within the teaching profession, a conclusion generally supported by Demaine (2001). The Bradford Race Review (Ouseley, 2001) has also recently pointed to the marginalisation of minority ethnic governors and teachers in schools as one of the divisions reflecting and contributing to poor race relations in the city.

The small numbers of minority ethnic students on teacher training courses, and the tendency for teachers from these backgrounds to be concentrated in lower-grade posts, was also mentioned.

> The majority of ethnic minorities were also found to have experienced discrimination and harassment during the course of their teacher training and following qualification. (Ouseley, 2001)

This seemed to suggest that matters have not significantly improved over the past decade since Siraj-Blatchford (1990) reported a study of 70 teacher training institutions in the UK. This found that the training received by minority ethnic group students very often undermined any positive expectations of teaching initially held:

> They reported experiencing direct and indirect racism within teacher-training establishments and on teaching practice: 40 per cent of minority ethnic group students reported experiencing 'racism' from initial teacher education (ITE)

lecturers, 64 per cent from fellow students and 60 per cent from staff and pupils in teaching practice schools.

The Teacher Training Agency (2000) has, in collaboration with bodies including the Commission for Racial Equality, Ofsted, LEA Advisers, and the Runnymede Trust, drafted 'Guidance and Resource Materials for Initial Teacher Training Providers' to raise the attainment of minority ethnic pupils. Among the issues discussed were: the ethos and practices of the school; an inclusive curriculum; effective language and learning support for pupils with English as an additional language (EAL); understanding cultural and religious issues; the early years; teaching refugee pupils; effective liaison with parents and other carers; effective links with the community; and good practice in the recruitment, retention and support of minority ethnic trainee teachers. These provide considerable scope for policy and practice developments within schools.

Supplementary schools

Supplementary and mother-tongue schools (popularly known as Saturday schools) have become established in Britain in response to concerns that mainstream education is failing to meet the needs of black children. Their origin lies in the early 1970s and the publication of Coard's (1971) influential booklet on the under-achievement of West Indian boys. It was argued that these pupils had low attainments in part because there were low expectations of them, and that they would thrive only in educational settings that valued their culture and instilled them with pride and self-confidence. Some supplementary schools were set up as a result, but on the whole developments at that date were slow.

By the early 1980s the movement had another advocate in Stone (1981) who wrote on the education of the black child in Britain. She was an early critic of multiculturalism and claimed that the belief that black children would do better at school only if they ceased to feel culturally isolated and hostile to school and teachers had meant that often:

> steel band sessions and West Indian dialect classes replaced basic skills, and among teachers 'relating to the kids' was valued over sheer teaching ability.

She called for a radical rethink of educational policies that recognised that children will succeed only if taught appropriate skills and knowledge. Her own study found that pupils receiving only a 'multicultural education' did less well than those also attending supplementary schools. Putting her conclusions starkly, she commented:

while schools try to compensate children by offering black studies and steel bands, black parents and community groups are organising Saturday schools to supplement the second-rate education which the school system offers their children.

The most rapid rise in supplementary schools was probably during the early 1990s and there are currently over a thousand in Britain. These are available to pupils from a range of backgrounds and at all academic levels. Richards (1995) indicated that most are for African-Caribbean children, although some may especially target pupils from Asian backgrounds. They are generally set up by community activists and depend on the local black population for staffing and resources. They tend to be characterised by strong parental links and community involvement.

Nagra (1981/2) pointed out that the specific aims of these schools may differ somewhat depending on the pupils who attend. Asian schools tend to place more emphasis on culture, religion and language, whereas those for African-Caribbean pupils focus more on basic skills. It seemed that:

> Asian schools may be more about opting out of mainstream education, whereas the African-Caribbean are more about helping pupils to achieve in the state system.

Okitikpi (1999) stressed their additional value as somewhere for pupils from similar backgrounds to meet socially, and in providing an opportunity to learn about black history which is outside the National Curriculum.

There has been little formal evaluation of supplementary schools. One recent study in the Lambeth Education Action Zone (Bastiani, 2000) reported almost entirely positive views from pupils and parents in relation to three schools. It concluded that they had an important role in helping to boost a child's sense of confidence, both academically and socially, and providing positive black images and role models. More evaluative work in this area would be valuable.

Supplementary schools are outside the state system and, until recently, most have existed with little funding. In the past, they appear to have valued their independence and rarely sought financial support from mainstream education. Their importance in providing for the special educational needs of pupils from black and minority ethnic backgrounds is, nonetheless, increasingly recognised, and £1 million from the Social Inclusion and Pupil Support Grant was allocated in 2000 to help develop links with mainstream schools. A new independent body is being set up to provide them with help and advice and to generate fundraising ideas. The scheme also recognises the contribution that parents and the community can make to the success of a school and the progress of its pupils and aims to encourage this in the supplementary schools.

Providing multicultural education

The history of multicultural education has run parallel to the development of supplementary education, and has been accompanied by similar debate and discussion. Fundamental to this has been the interpretation of multiculturalism. Does it emphasise differences at the expense of equality of opportunity or take a more egalitarian form and involve the recognition of cultural diversity coupled with equal opportunity in an atmosphere of mutual tolerance? Recent years have witnessed a shift from the former to the latter of these perspectives.

The Swann Report (1985) made an important early contribution to the discussion of this concept and its meaning for schools. Based on detailed reports from four local education authorities implementing policy in this area, it seemed that there was at the time no consensus on what multicultural education actually meant. In practice the focus was often on developing education for a multicultural and non-racist society without confronting the issue of equality of opportunity for the minority ethnic child. Rex (quoted in the Swann Report), in line with the views of Stone (1981) some years earlier, stressed the need for multicultural education to address all these needs simultaneously:

> The question of underachievement by an ethnic group or class is a real one in our schools, but its practical solution must lie in better educational practice rather than in emphasising the cultural and environmental differences between children outside the school.

The Swann Report attributed the absence of agreed and accepted aims and objectives for multicultural education to:

> the vagaries of political pressures in this field, at both central and local level, over the years

and also pointed to the need for multicultural education in 'all-white' schools despite the finding that:

> Almost without exception, the schools visited saw the concept of multicultural education as remote and irrelevant to their own needs and responsibilities, taking the view that such an approach was needed only where there were substantial numbers of ethnic minority pupils.

Although the seeds were thus sown for greater commitment to a broad-based definition of multicultural education, it was nonetheless some years before the debate really took off. It was a decade later when Gillborn (1995) reported on research looking at how some schools had sought to deal with race, racism and anti-racism, and emphasised the centrality of this component within multicultural strategies. This was followed by the publication of a series of key reports on the attainment of minority ethnic pupils (see above) which pointed to the need for schools to adopt a wide range of measures embracing both the promotion of awareness of ethnic diversity, and equality of opportunity and outcome for children whatever their background. The review of the national curriculum in England (Qualifications and Curriculum Authority, 1999) indicated that schools should provide for the diversity of pupils' needs, including the provision of support for pupils for whom English is an additional language.

Many of the main conclusions on multicultural education were brought together in a Department for Education and Employment (2000d) document that highlighted four specific areas to be addressed in raising achievement levels for minority ethnic pupils:

- encouraging high expectations among the pupils in question through, for example, mentoring programmes and potential role models;
- providing an appropriate culture and ethos in the school which includes school-wide values, high standards of behaviour and respect for others, fair systems of reward and reprimand, and measures to reduce stereotyping, prejudice and poor race relations;
- involving parents in their children's education and in school activities more generally; and
- monitoring attainments by ethnicity.

Most reports and reviews have acknowledged the existence of good practice, recognised that there is no single or simple formula for multicultural education, and urged greater efforts in this area. Most have also highlighted aspects found to be particularly important. Blair and Bourne (1998), for instance, made two specific recommendations:

> If we were to identify any significant additional and transferable key characteristics of effective schools, however, we would focus on two. Firstly, ... 'listening schools', schools which took time to talk with students and parents; schools which were prepared to consider and debate values as well as strategies; schools which took seriously the views students and parents offered their own interpretations of school processes; and schools which used this learning to reappraise, and where necessary change, their practices and to build a more inclusive curriculum. These

schools did not assume the existence of ethnic stereotypes or indeed of fixed ethnic identities, but recognised the shared experiences of students in their evolving, culturally diverse communities.

Secondly, that to effectively identify, target and meet changing needs in a dynamic, culturally and linguistically diverse context, schools needed the resources which would allow them to achieve at least a little flexibility in the deployment of their staffing.

The guidance offered by the Department for Education and Employment (1999a) pointed to successful initiatives to address both under-achievement and racial bullying and harassment. Circulars have stressed how so-called 'colour-blind' policies can encourage inequalities between ethnic groups and have highlighted the importance of monitoring by ethnicity for achievement and bullying:

governing bodies and teachers should monitor the use of sanctions against pupils of ethnic minority background and reassure themselves that the school's policy against racial prejudice and harassment is being fully enforced.

Clear strategies, documentation of all incidents and how they have been dealt with, and full reports to parents, governors and LEAs on the issue, are regarded as essential. All schools have been required to comply with this guidance since September 1999.

It is universally recognised that multicultural education presents difficult challenges. Ofsted (1999) acknowledged that schools do not always know how to deal with underachievement among minority ethnic pupils, and the Report of the Stephen Lawrence Inquiry (Macpherson, 1999) called for Ofsted to take a major responsibility for monitoring strategies in schools to prevent and address racism in education. Osler and Morrison (2000) have, however, suggested that Ofsted has not successfully taken on this role of inspecting schools for race equality. Based on an examination of Ofsted documents, interviews with senior Ofsted personnel, contracted inspectors, head-teachers and senior LEA officers, as well as a review of the literature, they concluded that:

race equality is not yet recognised as a central feature of educational inclusion by all at Ofsted.

This meant that monitoring by ethnicity and for racial harassment and bullying were not given priority, that:

the distinction between pupils with special educational needs and those for whom English was an additional language was not always clear ... [and that] prior to inspection, headteachers ... did not generally anticipate that equality issues in general, or race equality in particular, were likely to be a feature of inspection.

Multicultural education continues to be a priority in relation to raising the attainment of pupils from black and minority ethnic backgrounds, reducing levels of permanent exclusions from school, reducing racism, and promoting equality of opportunity and outcome. Among new government initiatives, the Schools Plus Policy Action Team 11 report on 'Improving the educational chances of children and young people from disadvantaged areas' (Department for Education and Employment, 2000e) has targets that relate directly to young people from minority ethnic backgrounds. Under the heading of 'Raising ethnic minority achievement', there are recommendations for the funding of supplementary and mother-tongue schools allied to the 'Schools Plus Team' proposal to help minority ethnic pupils in particular. In addition, 'an expanded programme of mentoring for pupils from ethnic minority backgrounds, offering qualifications through accreditation for mentors taking part in the programme' and the encouragement of all schools to use monitoring, evaluation and target-setting to help raise minority ethnic achievement, are among its aims. The introduction of Citizenship into the curriculum (see pages 159) is another significant development in relation to multicultural education.

Parekh (2000) included recommendations for education in its recent and widely publicised report. Among the issues highlighted were: the need for statistics on ethnicity together with guidance on how they should be used; attainment and exclusion among African-Caribbean children; initial and in-service training issues; the school curriculum; and the content and process of the school inspection system in relation to race equality and cultural diversity. Specifically, it was suggested that a forum should be set up to review educational developments in these areas.

Monitoring by ethnicity

There has not, in the past, been a requirement for schools to collect information on pupils' ethnic background. Nonetheless, an increasing number have, over recent years, gathered details from parents on entry to primary school, and again at transfer to secondary education, based on ethnicity categories used in the 1991 Census. Many gaps, however, remain. This was illustrated by Gillborn and Mirza (2000) who found that, even among the 118 authorities putting in applications for the Ethnic Minority Achievement Grant (EMAG), only two in three were able to provide information on attainment by ethnicity. Even where information is available, this usually provides school rather than individual pupil profiles and is therefore of limited value for monitoring by ethnicity. This was well illustrated by Blair and Bourne (1998) who clearly demonstrated how failing pupils could be 'hidden' if they attended schools with high attainment profiles.

The Department for Education and Employment (2000a) has now issued draft guidance for schools which it is hoped will, following consultation and implementation, lead to much more effective monitoring by ethnicity. This guidance emphasised the importance of ethnic monitoring in understanding different patterns of attainment[7] among ethnic groups and for exploring the role of determining factors such as: language skills, social class, neighbourhood, expectations by pupils and teachers, truancy and exclusions, and school ethos.

It proposed that from 2002 ethnicity will, in line with 2001 Census definitions, be recorded on all named pupil records so that individuals and not just school totals can be monitored through the Annual School Census. It is recommended that the information is collected from parents for those under 11, preferably from pupils for ages 11 to 15, and from pupils aged 16 or over. Details on ethnicity must not be recorded if the parent or pupil refuses to supply them, and all definitions provided by parents or pupils must be accepted. It remains to be seen to what extent this guidance is followed and whether pupil monitoring by ethnicity improves as a result.

Monitoring by ethnicity has also been called for in relation to other educational indices such as the occurrence of racist incidents and how they are dealt with, and staffing issues. There is clearly a long way yet to go.

Summary points

- There continue to be striking differences in average levels of attainment according to ethnicity, although exceptions are also reported.
- Boys from African-Caribbean and mixed-heritage backgrounds are at greatest risk of permanent exclusion from school.
- Teacher expectations and school processes can, even if not deliberately, disadvantage pupils from minority ethnic backgrounds, particularly those of African-Caribbean origin.

---

7 From 2001, annual primary and secondary school performance tables will not include pupils from overseas whose first language is not English and who were admitted to an English school for the first time on or after the start of Year 5 (for the primary school tables) or Year 10 (for the secondary school tables).

- A growing number of supplementary schools have been set up to meet the needs of minority ethnic pupils, but these lack formal evaluation.
- Multicultural education is in theory, although not necessarily in practice, strongly on the agenda.
- Proposals have been made for more systematic monitoring by ethnicity in schools, but it is not yet clear how far they will be carried out.

8. Moving on from Education

Compulsory education ends at 16 years after which pupils remain at school, move on to some other form of education, join a training course, get a job, undertake voluntary work, or begin a period of unemployment. Available statistics and evidence suggest that patterns of activity at this point of transition vary quite markedly according to ethnicity.

Making the choice

The best information on young people's patterns of education, training and employment after the age of 16 is derived from the Youth Cohort Study (YCS)[8]. This provides information on the situation of young people at 16 years as well as one and/ or two years later. Better information may become available in the next years as:

> The Department is planning a longitudinal study of the transition of ethnic minority young people from compulsory education through further and higher education into the labour market. This will inform us of the experiences and motivations contributing to young people's post-16 choices. (Pathak, 2000)

Quite striking differences by ethnicity were found on analysis of data from the first sweep of the YCS Cohort 10 in 2000 (Department for Education and Employment, 2001d). Although the majority of 16-year-olds remained in full-time education, patterns differed between groups. Young people in the white group were least likely to have stayed in full-time education (70 per cent) or to be studying for a qualification, and most likely to be in a government-supported training scheme or a full-time job (11 per cent). Seven per cent were not in any education, training or employment. The

---

8 Information is also available from the Career Activity Survey, undertaken by local Careers Services, which collects details annually on the destinations of young people completing Year 11. Although the survey is meant to cover all schools, its coverage is in practice patchy with the greatest non-response in inner London. Information on ethnic group was not provided for almost 15 per cent of the sample overall in 1998.

Indian and other Asian groups presented the greatest contrast, with the highest proportions still in full-time education (92 per cent of the Indians) and studying for a qualification, and the smallest proportions in government-supported training or a full-time job (3 per cent of the Indian and 1 per cent of the other Asian groups). The other Asian group had the lowest proportion (2 per cent) not in any education, training or employment. The Black, Pakistani and Bangladeshi groups came somewhere in between and, among those studying for a qualification, were the most likely to be aiming for a vocational level 1 or 2 qualification. Those of Bangladeshi origin were, furthermore, the group most likely (9 per cent) not to be in education, training or employment of any kind.

The findings from the third sweep of Cohort 9 (Department for Education and Employment, 2001c) confirmed this picture. By 18 years, young people from minority ethnic groups (69 per cent for these groups overall) were more likely than white young people (39 per cent) to be in full-time education.

Differences were less marked for higher education, with participation rates only slighter lower for young people from white (23 per cent) relative to minority ethnic (26 per cent) backgrounds. This latter figure, nonetheless, hid considerable variation in participation rates between members of the Indian group (34 per cent) at one extreme and those from Pakistani and Bangladeshi backgrounds (15 per cent) at the other. Of all the groups, white young people were the most likely to have full-time jobs or to be engaged in government-supported training. Few differences emerged in the proportions not in education, training or employment: these were around the 11 per cent level for both white and minority ethnic groups as a whole.

Fitzgerald and others (2000) reported a study of a representative group of 264 black Caribbean males aged between 18 and 30 years. Comparing rates with information from the Labour Force Survey, they confirmed the higher unemployment rate among this group compared to members of the white population, as well as the increased likelihood of employment in clerical, secretarial and sales jobs rather than managerial and professional positions. The Fourth National Survey of Ethnic Minorities (Modood and others, 1997) also found unequal unemployment rates and showed that these were independent of educational qualification. Black Caribbean graduates were, for example, more than twice as likely as white graduates to be unemployed.

The Runnymede Trust report (Parekh, 2000) also pointed to Labour Force Surveys which, over recent years, have consistently shown how Asian and black school-leavers are less successful in finding employment than their white peers, and how this remained true when factors such as educational attainment were taken into account.

Factors influencing patterns

An important, but unresolved, question concerns the reasons for these different patterns. A range of factors is likely to be contributory. Local patterns of opportunities are significant and there may, for example, be more possibilities for minority ethnic groups living in cities rather than elsewhere. The Social Exclusion Unit (1999) suggested that young people from minority ethnic communities can have greater difficulty finding places on training schemes and demonstrated how, in 1997, only 3.4 per cent of Modern Apprentices were black compared with a population benchmark of 8 per cent. Pathak (2000) called for more information on school admission policies for sixth-form courses in case these discriminated against lower-achieving students. Qualification levels are, furthermore, almost certainly influential. Fitzgerald and others (2000) indicated that relative success in the labour market seemed to be influenced by school record: those who admitted to playing truant were 52 per cent less likely, and those gaining GCSEs or higher qualifications were 108 per cent more likely, to have gained managerial and professional jobs. Qualifications alone, however, do not explain why both higher-achieving Indian pupils and lower-achieving Bangladeshi young people seem particularly likely to continue their education. Discrimination, too, probably plays a part. According to their own accounts, 62 per cent of the young men in Fitzgerald and others's sample said they felt they had been treated unfairly because of their skin colour, with 44 per cent and 32 per cent respectively saying this with specific reference to getting a job and how they were treated at work.

Berthoud (1999) presented some interesting and detailed comparisons of 'young' men from Caribbean and other backgrounds in the labour market based on Labour Force Survey data. Although his findings related in the main to older men, the sample did include males from 16 years old. The findings, moreover, may have applicability for all age groups.

The purpose of Berthoud's analysis was to interpret the widening gap in opportunities available to different minority ethnic groups and the relatively poor employment prospects facing those from Caribbean, Pakistani and Bangladeshi backgrounds. He argued that traditional explanations stressing the effects of migration and discrimination were not sufficient, and that culture and expectations were almost certainly important too. He suggested, for example, that family structure could have an impact, such as if in a Caribbean family there was no father-figure role model or if the mother was happy to support her son without assistance from social security. Outcomes might also be affected by both teacher and pupil expectations of lower attainment among certain minority ethnic groups. Education and achievement themselves were, moreover, important. A multiple regression analysis suggested that, compared with a white man, men and women from different groups needed the following number of extra years of education to achieve the same qualifications: white woman (1); Caribbean man (0.6); Caribbean woman (1.3); African man (1.1); African woman (1.4); Indian man (1.1); Indian woman (1.7); Pakistani/Bangladeshi man (1.9); and Pakistani/Bangladeshi woman (1.8).

Overall, it seemed that employment patterns were determined by a complex mix of qualifications, local unemployment rates, and cultural factors which varied according to ethnicity. Africans, for example, did not seem to benefit from education in the way that those from Caribbean backgrounds did – but would this still be the case if the latter achieved the educational levels of the former? An important conclusion Berthoud felt able to draw was that:

> there is no hint that the employment disadvantage observed among young Caribbean men is a temporary phenomenon which will disappear with the passage of time. The disadvantage is experienced by young men who were born and brought up in Britain, educated here and unemployed here. It will not go away until something is done about it.

Parekh (2000) confirmed that a number of reasons seemed likely to be important in determining employment patterns among young people, and that these went beyond racial discrimination. Citing recent studies he suggested that young people's own behaviour might in some way affect outcomes:

> In one recent study young people were conscious of the extra difficulties they faced or were likely to face when putting themselves forward for opportunities. This awareness constrained their job-seeking behaviour, so that again the very anticipation of rejection on racial or ethnic grounds meant that, over time, processes of exclusion continued to operate without individual acts of direct discrimination taking place.

Improving the job opportunities of young people from minority ethnic backgrounds would seem from the evidence to require a multi-faceted approach.

Promoting education and training

The New Deal initiative has set targets for equality of outcome for young people from minority ethnic groups to help to ensure that similar proportions of young people from different groups find jobs. Initial partnerships have been established in areas that include Bolton, Coventry and Wembley. Although this initiative is in an early stage, Parekh (2000) has suggested that it has not yet been successful in achieving its aim:

> The New Deal for 18 to 24 year-olds, which started in 1998, has so far produced significantly worse results for black and Asian young people than for white. The Modern Apprenticeships Scheme has recruited barely half the black and Asian trainers to be expected from their numbers in the age group.

Connexions (2000), the universal service provided to pupils at school, is also relevant to the high levels of school exclusion and low average attainment shown by pupils from minority ethnic groups as a whole. This programme is based on the provision of Personal Advisers for help and support and noted as a specific aim 'tackling poor achievement rates for ethnic minority pupils through the Ethnic Minority Achievement Grant'. One of its purposes is to encourage disadvantaged and disaffected young people to stay in education and training until the age of 18 years. The longer-term outcomes of programmes and initiatives such as this remain to be seen.

A recent Cabinet Office (2001) report has suggested that inequality between minority ethnic and white groups is likely to widen over the next decades unless direct action is taken. The operation of the labour market is seen as highly significant and the Performance and Innovation Unit has accordingly been asked to undertake a new project in this area. This will focus directly on the position of minority ethnic groups in the labour market in relation to their educational qualifications. It is hoped that recommendations will emerge for increasing the achievement of these groups in the labour market.

Summary points

- Young people from different ethnic groups show distinct patterns of education, training and employment upon reaching the end of compulsory schooling.
- There is evidence to suggest that young people from Asian and black minority ethnic groups have fewer employment opportunities than their white peers.
- It would seem that a range of factors influence activities during the immediate post-school years, but the inter-relationships between these factors are complex.
- The value of initiatives to promote equality of opportunity at this transition stage has yet to be demonstrated.

9. Physical Health

The report on an independent inquiry into inequalities in health (Acheson, 1998) and other studies have demonstrated significant health disadvantages for people from black and minority ethnic communities. As many ethnic groups in Britain also experience forms of social deprivation that interact with health inequality (Department of Health, 2000a) the reasons for these differences remain unclear. Spencer (1996b) tried to unravel 'race' and ethnicity in determining child health and concluded that poor outcomes seemed due more to adverse socio-economic circumstances than to any biological or cultural explanation. It is, nonetheless, apparent that:

> The lack of research evidence, and sometimes interest, in significant and important areas of black, Asian and ethnic minority health is a common theme in the research literature. (Alexander, 1999)

Health in infancy

Infant mortality rates have been found to be about one-and-a-half times as high for children whose mothers were born in the Caribbean or Pakistan rather than in England, although at comparable levels for those with mothers born in East Africa, Bangladesh or India (Office for National Staistics, 1997). Similar patterns have been demonstrated over at least the last ten years. Smaje (1995) suggested that the highest rates of all are found among poorer families from Bangladeshi, Pakistani and Caribbean communities.

To some degree, these infant mortality rates reflect the greater levels of congenital and constitutional anomalies found in some ethnic minority groups compared to the white indigenous population (Little and Nicholl, 1988; Webb, 1996). Although their causes are debated and unclear, such congenital abnormalities have been found to affect the mortality of Asian infants, particularly those from Pakistan, who also show increased mortality from perinatal conditions. Increased rates of death among West African and

Caribbean infants, by contrast, seem due more to perinatal conditions than to congenital abnormalities (Smaji, 1995). Low birthweight is also a risk factor for infant, particularly perinatal, mortality, and more common among infants born to mothers born on the Indian sub-continent, East Africa, West/South Africa and the Caribbean than those born in the UK (Raleigh and Balarajan, 1995).

It has also been suggested that higher rates of infant death, as well as inherited metabolic disorders, among the Pakistani group in Birmingham may be attributable to the large numbers of consanguineous marriages within this group. Statistics collated for the Birmingham Health Authority (reported by Haslam, 2001) indicated that infant mortality rates in the Pakistani community were almost three times higher than for any other group in Birmingham, and it appeared that consanguineous marriages, alleged to be common in the Muslim community, led to increased health risks.

> There's nothing wrong in marrying first cousins; as such, it doesn't give rise to anything. But if you're carrying a gene that you've inherited from an ancestor, and your partner comes from the same family and he has the same gene too, when you have children the genes find a pair and this allows certain groups of conditions, such as auto-recessive illnesses, to manifest metabolic conditions, such as phenylketonuria, galactosemia and cystinosis.

The report concluded that although the increased risk of congenital abnormalities was often put down to socio-economic conditions, it appeared that inter-relation marriages now had a greater impact. This is an issue that would merit further investigation.

Height, weight and obesity

The 1999 Health Survey for England[9] (Erens and others, 2001) has provided the most comprehensive health data on black and minority ethnic groups in Britain based on a survey of over 3,000 children and young people. Age for age, this found that boys and girls from black Caribbean backgrounds were significantly taller than those in the

---

9 The Health Survey for England is carried out annually by the Department of Health, with a particular focus on a different disease or condition or population group each year. In 1999 (Erens and others, 2001) the focus was on minority ethnic groups. Over 64,000 addresses were screened to see if they included members from black Caribbean, Indian, Pakistani, Bangladeshi, Chinese and Irish backgrounds, and interviews were carried out with over 5,000 adults and 3,416 children from these communities. Findings were compared with those from a general population sample selected from up to two children aged 2-15 years from about 6,500 addresses. Interviews were conducted with 1,842 children in this part of the sample. Generally parents answered for those up to 12 years, and those aged 13 years or more provided information themselves. Some direct information on smoking, drinking, and use of cycle helmets was also gathered for 8- to 12-year-olds. The Strengths and Difficulties questionnaire was used for all 4- to 15-year-olds. Some other data, such as blood samples, were also collected.

general population (by an average of 2.3 and 2.6 cm). Bangladeshi and Chinese boys and girls, and Indian girls, were significantly shorter. Black Caribbean boys and girls were also heavier than their general population counterparts. Bangladeshi boys, and Indian, Bangladeshi and Chinese girls, were significantly lighter. Mean BMI (body mass index) was higher for black Caribbean boys and girls, and for Indian boys, than for the general population.

General health

Responses to three questions from the 1999 Health Survey on general health among young people up to 15 years demonstrated some differences according to ethnicity. These suggested that longstanding illness was less common among black and minority ethnic groups than in the general population where it was particularly common among boys. It was lowest of all among Bangladeshi and Pakistani girls (11 per cent in each case), but high among black Caribbean and Irish girls (the latter with higher rates than general population girls). Illness or injury curtailing normal activities during the previous two weeks emerged as most common among Irish and general population girls and general population boys (14 per cent in each case) and least common for Bangladeshi boys and Chinese girls (5 per cent). Asked to rate their own health, 9 per cent of general population boys and 8 per cent of girls said it was fair, bad or very bad. Girls from the Indian (about 13 per cent) and Bangladeshi (around 11 per cent) groups were most likely to give these responses. For boys, the highest rates were found for Pakistanis and Bangladeshis (13 and 16 per cent respectively).

Asthma is the most common chronic childhood disease in Britain, and the 1999 Health Survey included questions similar to those used in the International Study of Asthma and Allergies in Childhood for 2- to 15-year-olds. It emerged that respiratory symptoms were more common among both boys and girls in the black Caribbean, Irish and general population groups than among those from Indian, Pakistani, Bangladeshi or Chinese backgrounds. Except for boys in the general population, a similar picture emerged for asthma diagnosed by doctors.

Health behaviour

The Health Survey for England also included questions on health and lifestyle, and in particular on smoking, alcohol and physical activity. Some differences by ethnicity were found.

Children aged 8-15 years reported directly on whether or not they smoked. Compared with the general population (19 per cent girls, 21 per cent boys), Irish girls were more likely, and South Asian and Chinese children much less likely, to say they had ever smoked. Black Caribbean young people were very similar to the general population in this respect.

Use of alcohol was reported similarly. Young people in all minority ethnic groups (except for the Irish – 36 per cent of boys and girls) consumed less alcohol than the general population (40 per cent of girls and 32 per cent of boys had drunk alcohol). Indian and Chinese children were much less likely to have drunk alcohol (from 8 per cent of Indian girls to 18 per cent of Chinese boys), and rates of alcohol use were lowest of all among Pakistani and Bangladeshi groups (only 1 or 2 per cent). Findings from the 1996 British Crime Survey[10] also showed that young people between 16 and 29 years from minority ethnic backgrounds were less likely to take drugs or drink alcohol than white young people (Ramsay and Spiller, 1997). The survey revealed that 46 per cent of the white group, but 31 per cent of the African-Caribbean group, 22 per cent from Indian backgrounds and 16 per cent of those from Pakistani or Bangladeshi backgrounds, said they had taken drugs.

Despite low levels of drug use among young members of minority ethnic groups, there is some evidence that patterns are changing over time. A study by the Blackburn Police (Bennetto, 2000) reported a threefold increase in illegal drug use among Asian young people, most of whom were 16- to 25-year-old males, over a four-year period. Although, in the main, it was the use of cannabis that increased, there was also some rise in heroin use. Despite this change, however, white young people still accounted for 80 per cent of arrests on drugs charges.

Questions on physical activity in the Health Survey for England revealed no marked differences between groups, although South Asian boys and girls were the least likely to have participated in sports and exercise for at least five minutes during the previous week.

Non-fatal accidents are in some senses an index of healthy behaviour. Findings from the Health Survey for England demonstrated that the highest rates of major accidents (where a doctor was consulted or a hospital visited) were found in the general population (31 per cent boys and 22 per cent girls) and black Caribbean (32 per cent

10 The British Crime Survey is based on information from randomly-sampled adults in private households. The 2000 Survey achieved a 74 per cent response rate and covered a nationally representative sample of 19,411 people in private households in England and Wales. A minority ethnic booster sample of 3,874 adults who said their ethnic origin was black, Indian, Pakistani or Bangladeshi were also included. The survey has been carried out every two years but will be conducted on an annual basis from 2001.

boys and 24 per cent girls) groups. Rates for Irish boys and Indian girls were also relatively high, but they were lowest of all for Bangladeshi and Chinese girls (8 per cent).

Sickle cell disease and thalassaemia

Certain medical conditions apply only to specific minority ethnic groups. Among black and minority ethnic groups, sickle cell disease affects mainly people of African or African-Caribbean origin, and thalassaemia occurs in the main to children of Asian parents originating from India, Pakistan and Bangladesh. Both of these inherited disorders involve abnormal haemoglobin in the body and lead young people to suffer episodes of pain and show delayed growth and development. Ahmad and Atkin (1996) noted that over 6,000 people from the ethnic communities in the UK have either childhood sickle cell disorders or thalassaemia syndromes. It has been widely reported that haemoglobinopathies have not been adequately recognised as a significant public health issue and have accordingly received a low priority within health research and health services (Anionwu, 1996; Streetly and others, 1997). There is also evidence of considerable disparity of sickle cell disease management within general practice (Smith-Wynter, quoted by Department of Health, 2000b). Recent improvements in services in this area owe much to community activity (Tovey and others, 2001).

(a) Sickle cell

Sickle cell is an inherited disorder caused by abnormal haemoglobin (which carries the blood's oxygen) whereby the red blood cells become fragile and break down, blocking the tiny blood vessels. It is a form of anaemia and symptoms include painful swollen joints, which can involve the hands and feet, backache, intermittent possibly severe abdominal pain, typically due to damage to the blood vessels in the spleen, and jaundice. Sickle cell related pain has been classified as an acute recurrent pain syndrome. Crises are difficult to anticipate and are very variable in quality, duration, location and severity. They may occur in any part of the body, although more frequently in the extremities and may be brief (less than one hour) or last for several days. Growth and normal development may be delayed.

Symptoms are rare before six months and then they are episodic. Children may be very pale but otherwise without symptoms between crises. Those with the mild form of the disease can have no symptoms and a diagnosis is possible only through a blood test. Treatment can include bed rest and analgesics to help ease the pain. Blood transfusion may be necessary if the disease becomes severe. Damage to the spleen can mean a heightened risk of infection, and antibiotics may be used on a long-term basis to prevent this.

There are some relevant considerations in relation to diet, exercise and smoking. Folic acid supplementation can be recommended for young people who do not have a diet rich in fruit and vegetables. A diet low in iron is also advisable as the body has a tendency to store rather than use iron. Additionally important is the need to avoid dehydration which can precipitate a crisis. Increased fluid intake is therefore encouraged during travel, in hot climates, or during exercise. Alcohol is, because of its dehydrating effects, generally discouraged. Other situations that can precipitate a crisis include cold and exhaustion. Young people with this disorder are also advised against smoking as this can cause the acute sickle chest syndrome.

(b) Thalassaemia

The UK Thalassaemia Society (undated Fact Sheet) reports that up to 23 babies are born with B(beta) thalassaemia major in the UK each year, and that up to one in seven Asians may be carriers of the recessive gene. Of these births, 79 per cent are to Asian parents originating from India, Pakistan and Bangladesh, but only 7 per cent to parents originating from the Mediterranean who are traditionally thought of as the main risk group. If both parents carry the gene for the disease (they would be mildly affected themselves), there is a one-in-four chance that any child they produce will be severely affected. However, it is further maintained that only 5 per cent of UK Asians are aware of thalassaemia and fewer still have undertaken tests to see if they are carriers.

Thalassaemia is caused by the production of abnormal haemoglobin in the body which leads the red blood cells to become fragile and break down. The spleen becomes enlarged as it tries to produce extra red blood cells. Symptoms in children emerge between about 6 and 12 months. An affected baby is likely to appear pale and listless and does not feed well, and growth is retarded in older children. Children and adults with only a mild form tend to have no symptoms except possible slight anaemia.

Treatment for thalassaemia in its more severe form includes blood transfusions, although these can result in an accumulation of iron in the body. Bone-marrow transplants are also sometimes carried out to re-establish the manufacture of haemoglobin, usually with younger children. On occasion the spleen is removed if it has become severely enlarged. On a daily basis, most children with B thalassaemia major still require subcutaneous desferroxamine and regular blood transfusions.

Complications of treatment can include iron overload and result in diabetes, growth failure, delayed or failed puberty, early menopause and osteoporosis.

The daily routine of young people with thalassaemia may be severely affected. Regarding diet, the UK Thalassaemia Society recommends avoiding animal foods that are rich in iron, such as liver and spleen, as well as some foods such as prunes, raisins and spinach that also contain iron. They note that it is also wise to avoid alcoholic drinks, or to drink them only moderately as the liver is specially vulnerable in thalassaemia because of the iron stored in it. Other dietary considerations include ensuring that folic acid lost as red blood cells break down is replaced quickly.

Use of health services

Two key issues for health services are, first, whether different ethnic groups use these to differing extents and, second, whether any difference in patterns reflects varying needs or levels of need on the one hand or differential access or accessibility on the other.

Available information does suggest different levels of contact with services. Some studies have indicated that families from minority ethnic groups may use health services less (Fatimilehin and Nadirshaw, 1994; Association of Metropolitan Authorities, 1994), and others have shown that contact with health and social services seems to decline after children leave school (Thomas and others, 1988). Studies have also found that parents from minority ethnic groups felt that they were not able to share information about the nature of the child's disability, or ways of receiving practical help, with professionals offering services (Baxter, 1989; Swain and Eagle, 1987a and b).

Use of health services by 20,473 children and young people under 20 years in relation to ethnicity and social class was examined from General Household Survey[11] data collected in 1991-94. It was found that:

> A child or young person's ethnic origin was clearly associated with use of general practitioner and hospital services, which could imply that children and young people from minority ethnic groups receive a poorer quality of health care than other children and young people. (Cooper and others, 1998)

---

11 The General Household Survey has been carried out annually since 1971. Information is collected from a sample of around 13,000 people living in private households in Great Britain. The survey uses face-to-face interviews and covers topics such as housing, unemployment, education, health and family information. The ethnicity of household members is recorded.

Specifically, it emerged that Indian children and young people were more likely to see a GP than any other group, and that black Caribbean, Indian and Pakistani or Bangladeshi young people were less likely to use hospital inpatient and outpatient services than those classified as white.

More recently, relevant evidence has been provided by the 1999 Health Survey for England. First, this showed that more Pakistani and Bangladeshi children than other groups had seen a GP in the previous two weeks. However, only for Indian girls and Pakistani boys (both 16 per cent) was this at a significantly higher rate than in the general population (11 per cent for boys and 9 per cent for girls). Patterns of hospital attendance also revealed some differences. Children, and particularly girls, from South Asian and Chinese backgrounds were least likely to have been to an outpatient clinic. For boys, rates ranged from 15 per cent among the Bangladeshi group to 31 per cent among the Irish, and for girls from 11 per cent among the Chinese to 24 per cent of the general population. Further enquiry indicated that around nine in ten children in the general population group had been to a dentist at some time. Those in all minority ethnic groups, but especially Pakistani and Bangladeshi children, were less likely to have ever visited a dentist. The reasons for last visits were more likely to be due to problems with teeth than for a routine check-up in all minority ethnic groups as compared with the general population. The only groups to have significantly higher rates of toothache in the past four weeks than in the general population (where the rate was 5 and 6 per cent of boys and girls) were Indian girls (12 per cent) and Irish boys (10 per cent). Finally, it emerged that children from Indian and Pakistani backgrounds were less likely than others to be taking prescribed medicine.

Differential use of health services is due, in part at least, to their inability to meet the needs of all groups. Slater (1993) reported on the experiences of families from different minority ethnic groups using the NHS. It was concluded that many families faced problems and that the issues requiring attention included a lack of information, language and communication, staff attitudes, play, religious beliefs and observances, naming systems, hair and skin care, food in hospital, and the availability of haemoglobinopathy services. Parekh (2000) also made a number of recommendations for improving health and welfare. Among these were monitoring by ethnicity, training issues for those employed in health and social welfare services, and the need to make sure there are enough interpreters, including a telephone interpreting service. Bardsley and others (2000) have reached similar conclusions.

It is apparent, and implicit in some of the evidence cited above, that underuse of services by minority ethnic groups can reflect a lack of knowledge of what exists. The availability of home nursing services for children (Mullix, 1998; see Department of

Health, 2000b) is a good example. A survey of families found that while the experience of home nursing services appeared similar to the white and minority group populations, families from these latter groups reported less awareness of the services, and more anxiety and conflict of choice when these were offered.

There are, nonetheless, examples of good provision, including haemoglobinopathy services, which effectively target minority ethnic groups. Some of these have been published in directories of initiatives relevant to particular black and minority ethnic groups (Department of Health, 1996; 1998 b, c and d) and bring together information on projects by health authorities, trusts, charities and voluntary organisations which address the cultural and linguistic needs of these communities. They include books and booklets, catalogues, conferences, projects, service provision, training resources and videos, and span a wide range of topics from diet to mental health to access to services. Directories have entries in English as well as other relevant languages.

Monitoring by ethnicity

A report by the London Regional Office of the NHS Executive (1999) drew attention to the limitations of ethnic monitoring in relation to health despite the fact that such monitoring has been mandatory for hospital in-patients since April 1995. The report claimed that 'It is a field which remains contentious, partially collected and poorly used', and pointed out that the new Electronic Patient Record and Electronic Health Records provide:

> a major opportunity to ensure that ethnicity is included as a relevant patient data field, and to improve the use of ethnicity as a variable in analysis. Audit and analysis programmes will need to be developed to demonstrate how the data can be used to improve services and access to services.

The report also suggested that, while not currently mandatory, monitoring by ethnicity should begin during primary care and that this information could then accompany patients through the health system without having to be collected anew each time a service is used. It was noted that some health authorities have sponsored projects on ethnic monitoring in primary care, but that these have so far remained as pilot projects.

Summary points

- Higher rates of infant mortality have been found among children from some minority ethnic groups than among white children.
- There is no really striking evidence of differences in physical health according to ethnicity, although conditions such as sickle cell disease and thalassaemia are relevant only to some minority ethnic groups.
- Evidence suggests that children from minority ethnic groups show different patterns of health service use.
- Monitoring by ethnicity in the health services shows considerable scope for improvement.

10. Disability and Special Needs

There is little evidence to suggest that patterns of disability and special needs vary markedly according to ethnicity, nor indeed that the impact of disability on families might depend upon such factors (Shah, 1995). Most studies carried out in this area have focused on service needs and availability and have pointed to the particular disadvantage of disabled children and young people from black and minority ethnic backgrounds.

Patterns of disability

Elevated rates of certain types of impairment and disability among some minority ethnic groups have, nonetheless, been suggested. An analysis of statistics carried out by Bradford Social Services Department (reported by Herbert, 2000), for instance, indicated that Asian children in the city were 17.5 times more likely to be born with neuro-degenerative conditions than children in the non-Asian community, three times more likely to suffer from deafness, and almost twice as likely to have cerebral palsy. Moreover, 34 Asian children, compared with 6 in the wider community, were listed in 1998 as suffering from neurological damage. Reasons for these differences are, however, unclear. While the genetic risks of consanguineous marriages may in part be responsible, it is likely that factors such as poverty, poor housing, lack of exercise and poor diet are also contributory.

Further information on patterns of disability comes from the Children in Need (CiN) Census (Department of Health, 2001a). Just under a quarter of the disabled children receiving services under the Children Act 1989 during a week in February 2000 were from black and minority ethnic groups. Of the overall total, 10 per cent were from Asian or Asian British backgrounds, 9 per cent of black or black British origin, 3 per cent from mixed backgrounds, and a further 3 per cent of 'other ethnicity'. The report commented:

A comparison of these figures with the ethnic breakdown for all children in need suggests that the proportion of disabled children with disabilities from Asian and Black families receiving services in these authorities is greater than is the case for children in need generally. Data from the CiN census has the potential to shed light on how ethnicity is related to the prevalence of certain disabilities and the take up of social services. It would not be appropriate to draw out detailed findings from the data in this sample so more will be said about this in the next Children Act Report when the results of the 2001 CiN census will be to hand.

The CiN Census data also made it possible to compare the backgrounds of children with single and multiple disabilities. It appeared that those of Asian or Asian British origin or in the 'other ethnicity' category were most likely, and those of mixed heritage least likely, to have more than one disability. These findings led the Department of Health (2001a) to conclude:

These figures suggest that Asian and 'other ethnicity' families tend not to receive services to the same extent as other ethnic groups when their children have a single or few disabilities. However families from these ethnic groups who have children with multiple disabilities *do* appear to receive services because they are proportionately more highly represented among children with four and more disabilities.

In general, there is little widely-reported evidence that different groups show different patterns of disability, although conditions of sickle cell and thalassaemia (see pages 68–70) have some relevance in this context. Shah (1995) has suggested that impairments in Asian children may be under-reported and sometimes undetected by parents. It would seem that the evidence on this question is not clear-cut.

Studies of disabled children and young people

There have been several studies of families with disabled children from black and minority ethnic backgrounds (Shah, 1995; Emerson and Azmi, 1997; Parker, 1998), but these generally lack comparative information for other groups.

One large-scale study with a white comparison group has, however, recently been carried out. Chamba and others (1999) looked nationally at almost 600 families from black African/Caribbean, Indian, Pakistani and Bangladeshi backgrounds who were caring for a severely disabled child. They adopted a similar methodology to an earlier study of mainly white families (Beresford, 1995) that had suggested greater disadvantage for the small proportion of black and minority ethnic families in the sample in terms of living conditions, access to support and unmet needs. Comparing the findings of the two studies confirmed that the minority ethnic families were most likely to have a low income and lack information on their child's condition and available services (often due to communication difficulties). Mothers were also more likely to receive low levels of support from their partners as well as the extended family. Housing problems were especially common for Pakistani and Bangladeshi families, and while two in three of the families said they would like short-term breaks from caring for their child, only one in four had received these. Overall, these minority ethnic families seemed to have higher levels of unmet need than the white families.

Similar conclusions have emerged from other studies. These have, for instance, pointed to the added difficulties facing carers of black children with disabilities seeking respite care (Robinson and Stalker, 1993; Prewett, 2000). Shah (1995) summarised some of the main difficulties for minority ethnic groups as:

> The barrier of inadequate information and lack of interpreters, the reluctance to offer some services such as respite care because of misunderstandings about the role of the extended family and the poor housing and poverty exacerbate any problems of care.

Emerson and Azmi (1997) found that many of the Asian carers in their sample did not know about available services: only about one in three could speak English and fewer could write it. Moreover, two-thirds of the carers had difficulties paying their bills and the majority seemed to be suffering from stress. Shah (1997) outlined ways in which services for Asian families with disabled children could be improved.

Older disabled young people

An interview study with 44 disabled people aged 16-30 years of Asian, African and Caribbean origin living independently in four areas has also been reported (Bignall and Butt, 2000). Most of these young people had learning difficulties but others were deaf or hard of hearing, had visual impairments or multiple disabilities. The majority relied on their families for support and few were in contact with social care agencies. There also seemed to be few opportunities for them to make informal contact with other young black disabled people to share experiences. Some of the deaf young Asians appeared to feel especially isolated: they may not have had a language in common with their family and did not understand their cultural practices and expectations. Religion was important to many of these young people who could not always take part in activities due to problems of physical access and communication. The authors reported that:

> Many spoke of being treated differently, although it was not always clear if they had been made to feel 'different' because of their ethnicity or because of their impairment.

Issues of policy and practice

The Disability Discrimination Act 1995 complements the Race Relations Act and the Equal Opportunities Act in protecting disabled children and adults from all ethnic backgrounds and with all disabilities from discrimination. The Disability Rights Commission, the Equal Opportunities Commission (EOC) and the Commission for Racial Equality (CRE), together with the implementation of the Human Rights Act, should ensure a new era of comprehensive and enforceable human rights for all disabled people. The Disability Rights Commission is committed to serving all communities and to ensuring that its helpline and other services are fully accessible in a range of community languages.

The Disability Rights Task Force Report (1999) acknowledged the CRE proposals for changes to legislation as well as the publication of the Stephen Lawrence Inquiry report and reported that the Task Force had:

> welcomed the Government's commitment to extending the Race Relations Act to cover all public services and ... made a number of recommendations to ensure that the public sector promotes equalising opportunities for disabled people. [It had] also considered measures to combat institutional discrimination on the grounds of disability.

Local authorities may, however, not always accord a priority to disability in relation to minority ethnic group membership. This was certainly suggested by Kahn's (2001) analysis of Year 2 Quality Protects Management Action Plans which examined how far the needs of disabled children and young people in black and minority ethnic communities were met. It was concluded that no valid assessment could be made as few local authorities specifically provided any information on the question. O'Neale (2000) also pointed out that black children with disabilities were particularly neglected:

> But there was a group of children for whom there was little provision for their various needs; this was black children with disabilities. Suitable local placements

were generally difficult to find, but issues of personal care, culture, religion and diet needs to be addressed in addition to issues of disability.

The issue of ethnicity also appears not to be a priority for the assessment of special needs as statistics of education do not present numbers of pupils with statements of special educational needs by ethnic group.

A national strategy

A new national learning disability strategy (Department of Health, 2001e) has recently set out how the government will provide opportunities for children and adults with learning disabilities, based on the four key principles of rights, independence, choice and inclusion. A Development Fund will be used for various developments including integrated facilities for children with severe disabilities and complex needs, as well as an Implementation Support Fund for advocacy, and a new national information centre and helpline for parents and carers. The government's objective is to ensure that disabled children gain maximum benefits from educational, health and social care opportunities, and that the transition to adulthood runs smoothly.

To ensure that disabled people from minority ethnic groups were properly represented within its recommendations, the Department of Health commissioned a report on learning difficulties and ethnicity (Ghazala and others, 2001). This drew the following four main conclusions:

- support groups in minority ethnic group communities can act as gateways to a range of services for disabled people and their families;
- more bilingual staff and interpreters are needed to improve communication and access to services;
- service providers need accurate and ongoing information from and about minority ethnic communities to meet their needs adequately; and
- better information is needed on the views of disabled people themselves within the different minority ethnic communities.

As part of an ongoing emphasis on user involvement, empowerment and participation, service users must be given a positive role in shaping and developing services, and it is essential to recognise both the diversity of minority ethnic groups and that views may differ between generations with different cultural attachments and expectations.

Summary points

- There is some limited evidence to suggest differences, although not marked differences, in patterns of disability according to ethnicity.
- Studies have also indicated greater disadvantage among black and minority ethnic families than white families with disabled children.
- National statistics that include both disability and ethnicity among young people are generally lacking.
- National strategies have begun to address issues relating to the development of appropriate services for disabled young people, including those from minority ethnic groups.

11. Mental Health

On the whole, there would seem to be greater concern about the mental health than the physical health of members of minority ethnic groups. Some differences between groups of children and young people have been demonstrated, both in patterns of difficulties and in access to services. A general lack of information in this area, however, means that it is difficult to draw firm conclusions on such patterns or their meaning. The whole area is one that warrants further investigation.

Psychological health

An elevated risk of behavioural, emotional or relationship difficulties among some, but not all, groups of children from minority ethnic backgrounds has been suggested (Erens and others, 2001). The Strengths and Difficulties questionnaire, designed to detect such difficulties, was administered to children between 4 and 15 years as part of the 1999 British Health Study. Among the general population sample, scores signifying possible emotional and behavioural difficulties were gained by 12 per cent of boys and 8 per cent of girls. Overall, the highest levels were achieved by Pakistani boys (22 per cent) and Pakistani, Indian and Irish girls (17, 16 and 14 per cent respectively).

Young people between the ages of 13 and 15 years were also asked to complete the GHQ12, a version of the General Health Questionnaire designed to detect possible psychiatric morbidity. No real differences in scores were found between the general population and the minority ethnic groups. Girls scored higher than boys, suggesting more difficulties, in each group.

The prevalence of three common childhood mental health conditions within different ethnic groups has recently been examined in the first population based national survey in the area (Meltzer and others, 2000). Rates of conduct disorders (awkward, troublesome, aggressive, and antisocial behaviours), emotional disorders (anxiety, depression and obsessions), and hyperactivity (inattention and overactivity), as well as less common disorders, were assessed from a survey of over 10,000 5- to 15-year-olds carried out in 1999 in England, Scotland and Wales. Information was collected from parents, children and teachers, and ethnicity was classified as white (91 per cent of the sample), black (3 per cent), Indian (2 per cent), Pakistani and Bangladeshi (2 per cent), and other groups (3 per cent). Overall, black young people were the most likely to have a mental disorder, and those classified as Indian, followed by the Pakistani and Bangladeshi group, least likely. In general, boys were more likely than girls to have a disorder, as were 11- to 15-year-olds relative to 5- to 10-year-olds. Among the black group, perhaps the most striking finding was that more than one in five 11- to 15-year-old boys had a disorder of some kind, and for 17.8 per cent this was a conduct disorder (compared with 8.6 per cent of the white boys in this age group, 2.3 per cent of the Indian group, 4.6 per cent of the Pakistani and Bangladeshi group and 7.2 per cent of the other groups).

Earlier investigations have also indicated higher rates of behaviour problems at school, conduct disorders, autism and schizophrenia among young people from African-Caribbean backgrounds attending clinics (Wolkind and Rutter, 1985; Goodman and Richards, 1995). Less symptomatology for Asian children has been reported in some (Hackett and others, 1991) but not all (Stern and others, 1990) studies.

More recently, Kramer and others (2000) looked at the ethnicity of patients referred to the Child and Adolescent Psychiatry clinics at St Mary's Hospital during 1991-2. Of the 252 (out of 355) young people on which there was information, 40.4 per cent were white UK, 15.3 per cent white non-UK, 18.6 per cent mixed ethnicity (12 per cent one UK parent and 6.6 per cent no UK parent), 9.8 per cent black, 7.7 per cent Asian and 8.2 per cent other. The proportions of clinic attenders from both white and non-white backgrounds appeared representative of the local population.

Findings contrasted sharply with those from studies suggesting higher levels of conduct disorders among African-Caribbean boys, as no apparent differences emerged between the white and the non-white sample in terms of school reports of behaviour, emotional or learning problems. Significant differences were, however, found in the referral agent and referral problems. Non-white children were more likely to have been referred by primary care health services, or to have referred themselves, and less likely to have been referred by secondary (e.g. paediatric) clinics. Fewer had disruptive disorders or were referred for developmental problems (although more were diagnosed with developmental disorder), and poor parenting often seemed to be the reason for referral. There was also a trend for non-white children to have more somatic disorders such as headaches, abdominal pain, chronic cough, fatigue and weakness. The similar levels of service use found for young people from Asian and other backgrounds were contrary to the findings of Stern and others (1990).

All these findings should, however, be viewed with caution. It has been questioned whether a mental health framework developed in the West is relevant to minority ethnic groups of non-Western origin (Littlewood, 1992; Jadhav, 1996). Among the issues raised by this debate are whether the assessment tools are appropriate, whether a lack of professional understanding about client culture, norms and values could result in a wrong diagnosis, and whether client understanding of mental health and mental health services, in combination with professional awareness of client need and the availability of suitable services, influences referral to services as well as their take-up. There may also be differences in cultural attitudes both about what constitutes a mental illness and also towards acknowledging the presence of mental illness within the family. Hodes and others (1998) wrote:

> Service use may also be influenced by earlier experience of a different organisation of health services in countries from which patients originate . . . . Additionally, parental concern about their child's behaviour influences referral to secondary psychiatric services. Service use will, therefore, also be affected by varying perceptions between parents of different ethnic backgrounds e.g. Thai, Jamaican and Gujarati parents are less tolerant of undercontrolled behaviour.

Suicide and deliberate self-harm

It is commonly claimed that rates of suicidal behaviour and deliberate self-harm are particularly high within Asian populations, and especially among women. These conclusions are based in part on studies that have shown that some groups of Indian women are at a much higher risk of suicide than either those of Bangladeshi or Pakistani origin, or the general population of England and Wales (Soni Raleigh and others, 1990; Soni Raleigh, 1996). It is important to note, however, that these studies were based only on women born in the Indian sub-continent. Investigations of broader population groups are less conclusive. One study of Asian and white patients admitted to a Birmingham hospital for self-poisoning did find significantly higher rates of referral among the former, but this difference was not found for either males or females under 24 years (Merrill and Owens, 1986). A more recent report has, on the other hand, indicated that rates of suicide among 15- to 24-year-old Asian women in Wolverhampton in 1993 were more than twice the national levels.

Suicide statistics do not currently record ethnicity and make it difficult to ascertain clear patterns. It has, however, been proposed by the National Service Framework on Mental Health that age, gender and race are in future recorded in this context (Jacobson, 2001). Better information on the links between suicide and background should accordingly become available.

There is also a lack of clear evidence linking ethnicity to the risk of self-harm among young people. One study of 64 white and 28 black adolescents referred to the psychiatric service of a London hospital (Goddard and others, 1996) found that referral rates were proportional to the respective populations in the locality. The two groups were, moreover, similar in terms of social and demographic factors, psychiatric symptoms, circumstances of the self-harm episode, and outcome. The main difference between the groups was that the black adolescents reported more social stress. Another study also reported no significant differences between Asian and caucasian females and self-harm (McGibben and others, 1992). Similar conclusions were drawn from a West London study (Bhugra, undated) of all adolescents presenting at a general hospital following deliberate self-harm: there was, again, no evidence to suggest higher rates among the Asian than the white group. Some interesting findings did, however, emerge. First, members of the Asian group did not report any regrets for their actions whereas two-thirds of white females did; and second, 61 per cent of white females but 42 per cent of Asian females reported low self-esteem.

Neeleman and others (2001) reported an interesting study carried out between 1994 and 1997 in which the relationship between ethnic density and deliberate self-harm was examined within 73 electoral wards in south-east London. The investigation was based on 1,643 people attending casualty departments for deliberate self-harm and looked at risk in relation to the representation of minority ethnic groups within their local area. Although relating to all age groups, the findings throw some light on the role of ethnicity in patterns of mental health. Rates were high in some areas, but low in others, which suggested that local density rates were in some way contributory to the risk of deliberate self-harm. In other words it looked as though contextual ethnicity rather than ethnicity itself was responsible for the prevalence rates found.

The Children Act Report 2000 (Department of Health, 2001d) noted that the ONS survey of mental health among children and adolescents in Great Britain (Meltzer and others, 2000) will publish findings of a further analysis of children who have harmed themselves. More information on the question of self-harm and ethnicity may, therefore, shortly be available.

Mental health services

The national service framework for mental health (Department of Health, 1999b) drew attention to evidence suggesting that services do not adequately meet the needs of minority ethnic groups and that black and minority ethnic communities lack confidence in the mental health services. This did not specifically address the needs of children and young people, but it pointed to the particular vulnerability of refugees and asylum seekers, and noted how the stigma attached to mental illness can be compounded by racial discrimination. It also referred to the high rates of psychotic illness among young males in the African-Caribbean population, and to the reputedly high rate of suicide among young Asian women. The Department of Health (1998e) strategy on modernising mental health services outlined how steps are being taken to address the particular mental health needs of minority ethnic groups, including the establishment of a number of local schemes (such as the Asian Family Counselling Services and the African Caribbean Mental Health Association) to provide services for specific groups.

The gaps and limitations in mental health services for young people from diverse backgrounds have been commonly cited (e.g.Mental Health Foundation, 1995). O'Neale's (2000) review of services for young people noted:

> The health and educational needs of ethnic minority children were in the main addressed, although there were gaps in child and adolescent mental health services and psychological support in most councils.

Kopraska and Stein (2000) pointed in particular to the major gaps in our knowledge concerning the mental health needs of looked after children and young people in relation to gender and ethnicity. Some authors and reports have detailed specific service difficulties. Yee and Au (1997), for instance, outlined how the British mental health services often fail to take cultural perceptions, including symbolic and belief systems, into account in working with Chinese families. The Commission for Racial Equality (1991) cited examples where needs were not being met which included an Asian patient being given a section of the Mental Health Act 1983 which he could not read, and hydrotherapy for Muslim women who are not allowed to appear in public in swimwear.

It is clear that more information on the one hand, and appropriate policy and practice developments on the other, are called for in all these areas.

Monitoring by ethnicity

There is little monitoring by ethnicity in relation to mental health issues. Kramer and others (2000) discussed the types of information that would be especially valuable in providing a child and adolescent psychiatric service and pointed out how these go beyond 'physical attributes and/or place of birth, health staff perception, or self-assignment'. Details, such as birth place of the child and parents, language used at home, religion, and whether the child is from a mixed-heritage background (Hodes and others, 1998), can be highly relevant.

Summary points

- Population studies have revealed some, although not marked, differences in mental health among young people from different ethnic backgrounds.
- The appropriateness of currently-used mental health assessment techniques for some minority ethnic group children and young people has been questioned.
- There is a lack of clear evidence to support or refute the view that rates of suicide and self-harm are generally elevated among young females of Asian origin living in Britain.
- There are widespread calls for improvements to mental health services for young people from minority ethnic backgrounds.
- The need for better monitoring by ethnicity is an issue in this as in other areas.

12. Physical and Sexual Abuse

Defining child abuse is not straightforward, and difficulties are compounded in any comparison of rates between groups with different ethnic and cultural backgrounds. The Social Services Inspectorate (1995) observed:

> There are within society wide ranging views about what constitutes child abuse. Different ethnic and cultural groups will be influenced in their views and responses by their own religious beliefs and cultural traditions as well as their values and attitudes to family and community life.

This, as has often been claimed, can relate to patterns of family discipline. Thoburn and others (1995), for example, pointed out how disagreements over appropriate physical punishment are common among cases involving black families in the child protection process. There is, nonetheless, no clear evidence on whether or not parents from some minority groups are more likely than others to use severe physical punishments, and certainly none to indicate that they are less likely to know the difference between punishment and abuse. This is the line taken by the Department of Health (2000a) that maintained that black and white families both support and reject smacking as a form of discipline and also took the view that:

> Culture can explain the context in which an abusive incident took place, but not the behaviour or action of an individual parent.

Patterns of abuse

At present, there are no official statistics on the incidence of physical and sexual abuse according to ethnicity. The National Society for the Prevention of Cruelty to Children also does not report any such information. The Department of Health will, however, include information on ethnic origin based on 2001 Census categories for children and young people on child protection registers for the year ending 31 March 2001.

The revised recording will also collect additional details on the enquiry processes that precede registration.

The best evidence currently available on patterns comes from smaller studies and surveys. Although this does not present consistent messages (see Creighton, 1992; Madge, 1997), and is not always based on British samples (Finkelhor,1986; Jones and McCurdy, 1992), it does on the whole suggest few differences between groups. Some distinctions in the most common types of abuse have, however, been reported. Gibbons and others (1995) found that while referral rates for the three broad groups were largely as expected, black and Asian families were more likely than white families to be referred for physical injury but less likely to be referred for sexual abuse. As almost half of the allegations appeared subsequently to be unsubstantiated, these findings do, none-theless, say more about patterns of referral than about the incidence of abuse itself.

It has been suggested by an NSPCC report (Gallagher, 1998) that some paedophiles may especially target members of black and minority ethnic groups:

> some ethnic minority communities and young people from poor backgrounds are seen as ripe territories for exploitation by paedophiles.

As these children might be presumed to be poor and to have language difficulties, it might also be thought that they would be unlikely to tell and would not make good witnesses in court. There might, in addition, be awareness of cultural pressures on members of some minority ethnic groups not to disclose abuse if it occurred.

Female genital mutilation is commonly regarded as a form of child abuse in its own right. Although against the Prohibition of Female Circumcision Act 1985, this practice is known to occur in Western countries including Britain. Reliable information on its extent is, however, lacking and systematic prevalence studies would be difficult to carry out (Dorkenoo, 1994). It is, accordingly, imperative that local agencies are aware of the possibility of female circumcision among the ethnic minority communities that practise it, and that whatever possible is done to prevent it.

Access to services

There appears to be widespread concern that sexual abuse may be particularly likely to remain undetected among black and Asian families. Gibbons and others (1995) indicated that the referral rate might be 20 per cent among these groups as compared with 31 per cent for white families. Moghal and others (1995) reached a similar conclusion from a study of sexual abuse within an Asian community and reported that:

Asian children were more likely to present in ways in which the professional needed a higher index of suspicion regarding the possibility of sexual abuse. Professionals may be less keen to act where Asian children are concerned unless they are sure of their facts.

Race (1999) indicated much the same in Bradford where it seemed that professionals were wary of intervention lest they be accused of racism. She confirmed the conclusion of the National Commission of Inquiry into the Prevention of Child Abuse (1996) that:

> The way culture, ethnicity and race combine to create a complex dynamic in child protection work is a major issue for consideration in relation to practice with black families.

Some of these issues were discussed by Chand (2000) who suggested that black and minority ethnic children and young people might be both more and less likely than others to be investigated for the possibility of child abuse. On the one hand, the 'pathologising' of black families can mean that their cultures and lifestyles are regarded as 'inherently problematic and need correcting' (Singh, 1992) and that unnecessary intervention takes place. On the other hand, however, 'cultural relativism' (Channer and Parton, 1990), which posits that all cultures should be judged according to their own standards, prevails with professionals uncertain when to intervene. Chand (2000) outlined some of the distinctions between families from different cultures which could be misconstrued in a child protection context. These fell within each of the seven categories of need (basic physical care, affection, security, stimulation of innate potential, guidance and control, responsibility, and independence) described in the 'orange book' which in the past has provided official guidance for social workers involved in child protection.

The Department of Health (2000a) has suggested that some black children may not be offered proper protection 'out of a fear on the part of white workers of being accused of racist practice'. The cases of two children, Tyra Henry (London Borough of Lambeth, 1987) and Sukina Hammond (The Bridge Child Care Consultancy, 1991), who died as a result of abuse by a father or step-father, were given as evidence of racism affecting practice and leading to a failure to intervene in situations where children were at evident risk of significant harm. The guidance described how:

> Racial and cultural stereotyping of black families can lead to inappropriate interventions in families as well as a failure to protect black children from abuse.

Farmer and Owen (1995) addressed the issue of minority ethnic families within the child protection system by observing 120 initial case conferences in two local authorities, and following up 44 cases registered over a two-year period, 10 of which involved children from minority ethnic backgrounds. They discussed the dangers of cultural stereotyping in assessing need when assumptions, such as likely support from the extended family, were made. This particular assumption was indeed frequently wrong, a conclusion also indicated by Berthoud (2000) (see page 26). Other erroneous assumptions were based on cultural mores and on the acceptability of different behaviours, such as a son sleeping with his father or the physical punishment of teenage rebellion.

These authors reported how many black families did not receive the services they needed, either before or after registration. Other research has also shown how families from some minority ethnic backgrounds use family support services to a lesser degree than other families (Butt and Box, 1998; Qureshi and others, 2000). This can mean, as Farmer and Owen (1995) noted, that a child's first contact with social services might be through the child protection system. As they suggest, such a situation is 'particularly unfortunate'.

There is, in conclusion, a need to ensure the availability and take-up of preventative services, such as family support, for families at risk to minimise the need for contact with the child protection system. Appropriate supplementary services must also be provided for families for whom this is not sufficient. The type of service most suitable for a particular family may not, however, always be easy to ascertain. While not able to offer any universal guidelines, Jackson (1996) discussed some of the special perspectives that may be relevant to the black experience of child sexual abuse. His main concern was how racism could affect the provision of support and care for the abused black child, and how it might prevent disclosure of abuse by these children. What, he asked, can we as a society do to redress the balance?

Monitoring by ethnicity

The issue of monitoring child abuse by ethnicity is an important one for child protection services, and the forthcoming statistics on the ethnicity of children on child protection registers are to be welcomed. Although a difficult task, it is also particularly important that monitoring is undertaken in such contexts as residential and foster care where concern is frequently expressed about the invisibility of abused black and Asian children. Utting (1997) reported that black children have been identified as a group particularly likely to be abused and harmed when living away from home.

Summary points

- While there may be differences in patterns of family discipline according to background, there is clear consensus on what constitutes abuse.
- At present there is limited information on detected abuse in different ethnic groups. This should change with the imminent inclusion of statistics on the ethnicity of children and young people on child protection registers.
- There is concern that physical and sexual abuse may remain undetected to a greater degree among minority ethnic than white children.
- Some evidence also suggests that minority ethnic families may be less likely than others to receive the services they need when abuse is suspected.

13. Youth Crime and Youth Justice

It is always difficult to ascertain patterns of youth offending with any certainty. A conviction for an offence depends not only on the committal of that act, but also detection of the crime and prosecution for it. Crime rates, accordingly, are in a sense a reflection of the whole criminal process. Determining youth offending by ethnicity is particularly difficult as the influence of institutional racism and differential treatment according to skin colour and background may be additional factors affecting statistics. Understanding the circumstances of racially aggravated crime is also complex and beyond the scope of this chapter.

Patterns of offending

Official statistics, covering a wide range of offences, and based on returns from Youth Offending Team managers to the Youth Justice Board in June 2000, have suggested some differences by ethnicity in patterns of offending (Home Office, 2001a). As shown in Table 13.1, young people from black and minority ethnic groups were overrepresented in each crime category considered, and this was particularly marked in the case of robbery. Disregarding instances where the ethnicity of the offender was unknown, it emerged that young people of black or black British origin were far more numerous than their representation within the total population group. Thus for robbery there were almost twice as many black or black British as white offenders despite a relative frequency within the population of about one to ten. This striking overrepresentation was not found for the other minority ethnic groups.

The meaning of crime statistics such as these depends on the operation of the youth justice process including the detection of offences and the extent to which these result in prosecution. Self-report data can provide a rather different picture and may be assumed to be a more reliable indicator of offending. There have, however, been few recent studies of this kind. One conducted several years ago (Graham and Bowling,

Table 13.1 Youth offending England and Wales, 1 April 2000 to 30 September 2000: (selected categories only) (%)

	white	mixed	Asian or Asian British	Black or black British	Chinese/ other	Unknown
violence against person (total of 4017)	58.8	1.3	3.4	15.6	1.4	19.5
robbery (N=1289)	29	1.7	6.3	43.2	1.2	18.6
burglary (N=1869)	66.5	1.3	2.9	10.2	1.7	17.4
vehicle theft (N=2293)	65.1	1.4	3.7	14.1	1.4	14.3
racially aggravated violence (N=194)	65.5	1	2.6	8.2	0	22.7

1995) confirmed differences by ethnicity. While 43 per cent of black and 44 per cent of white 14- to 25-year-olds said they had committed an offence in 1992, this was the case for 30 per cent of Indians, 28 per cent of Pakistanis and 15 per cent of Bangladeshis. All groups were most likely to report property offences. The most marked differences between groups occurred for violent offences: these were mentioned by one in four black young people, compared to less than one in five of both Pakistani and white young people, and less than one in ten Bangladeshis. Black young women were more likely than those in the other groups to admit an offence.

The interpretation of crime rates by ethnicity is far from straightforward. In general, links have been found between young offenders and a wide range of background factors from poverty and deprivation on the one hand to a lack of parental discipline and broken homes on the other (Farrington, 1996; 1997). However, although many young people from minority ethnic backgrounds come from low-income households, and high proportions from African-Caribbean backgrounds live in lone-parent families, there is no clear evidence on whether similar or different links between offending and background are found by ethnic group.

Nonetheless, it is important to take certain population characteristics of minority ethnic groups in Britain into account when examining patterns (Rutter and others, 1998). The younger age structure of these groups, and hence the disproportionate number of young people from minority ethnic backgrounds in the population, is one important factor. The tendency for these groups to live in cities and industrial towns, where crime rates are higher, is also important. This will have a bearing on their risk of becoming involved in criminal activities. Rutter and others (1998) also stressed the need to recognise how members of Asian and African-Caribbean rather than white ethnic groups are much more often the victims of most categories of crime. They reported, nonetheless, that the limited evidence on the question suggested that crimes of assault were more likely to be within than between ethnic groups.

Arrest and prosecution

Statistics on race and the criminal justice system (Home Office, 1999) have shown that a greater proportion of people from minority ethnic groups than from the white population are arrested and that there are differences between ethnic groups in the offences for which they are arrested. Nonetheless, after controlling for a range of factors such as the seriousness of the crime, record of offences, and admission of guilt, ethnicity did not seem to be a significant predictor of subsequent decisions (Home Office, 1998).

Analysis of 5,500 defendants aged under 22 years, whose cases were dealt with by the Crown Prosecution Service over a two-month period during 1996, did, however, indicate that those from minority ethnic groups were less likely than others to receive convictions (Barclay and Mhlanga, 2000). It was found, on average, that 78 per cent of white defendants, compared with 68 and 69 per cent of Asian and black defendants respectively, received convictions. Members of Asian groups were most likely to have charges against them dropped at an early stage because of lack of evidence, and once at a magistrates' court or the Crown Court both black and Asian defendants were more likely than white defendants to be acquitted. Black defendants were the most likely to plead not guilty at magistrates' courts.

When people of all ages are considered, those from minority ethnic backgrounds are more likely than those from white backgrounds to be stopped and searched by the police. Although the data are not available to corroborate this, it is likely that this is as true of young as older people. Statistics on race and the criminal justice system (Home Office, 1999) indicated that around one million people were stopped and searched in 1998-9 and that of these 9 per cent were black, 5 per cent were Asian and 1 per cent fell within the category 'other non-white'. Overall, black people were six times as likely as white to be stopped and searched. A study by FitzGerald (1999) for Scotland Yard suggested that the Metropolitan Police were still abusing their powers of stop and search. The implication was that this was increasing levels of antagonism by young black and minority ethnic young people towards the police.

Returns from Youth Offending Teams to the Youth Justice Board in June 2000 confirmed some of these findings. Statistics suggested that young offenders from minority ethnic groups are more often prosecuted than their white counterparts, slightly more likely to be allowed bail, and more likely to receive a custodial sentence:

> Young people from the minority ethnic communities receive eleven percent of the overall sentences imposed while receiving nineteen percent of the custodial sentences.

A NACRO (1999) report recently summarised the situation over recent decades, drawing on FitzGerald's (1993) review of research. This suggested that African-Caribbeans, especially young people, were more likely to be stopped by the police than whites, more likely to be arrested, less likely to be cautioned, and less likely than Asians to have no further action taken against them. They were also likely to face a different pattern of charges from those brought against whites or Asians, more likely to be remanded in custody, and more likely to plead not guilty to the charges against them. In addition they were more likely to be tried at Crown Court, more likely to be acquitted, and likely to receive more and longer custodial sentences, if found guilty, and a different range of non-custodial disposal. It is an interesting statistic that 51 per cent of young black males in Leicestershire had been arrested during the course of 12 months in 1995 (FitzGerald and Sibbitt, 1997).

Initiatives to reduce youth offending

A wide range of initiatives exists to deter young people from crime, and these are often targeted in areas of relative deprivation and disadvantage. Generally speaking they are focused on young people in general rather than those from specific ethnic backgrounds. Much of the work of the Social Exclusion Unit and the Policy Action Teams (Cabinet Office, 2000a) is relevant in this context.

The Youth Justice Board has also been responsible for much activity in this area. This has, for example, established the Mentoring Plus scheme, which is targeted at hard to reach minority ethnic and other young offenders. The scheme has been set up in partnership with *The Voice*, the African-Caribbean newspaper, and has the objective of providing adult role models to support young people through their community sentences, help them to re-enter school, training or seek employment and reduce offending behaviour. Additional funding is also being provided to tackle literacy and numeracy problems among 10- to 17-year-olds through learning mentors. This is in line with the premise that many young offenders have poor educational achievement and are unable to progress into training or employment as a result.

The work of Youth Offending Teams (YOTs) is relevant, in relation to the above and other activities. These include a strong focus on minority ethnic groups and have been shown (Youth Justice Board website, 2001) to be ahead of targets set by the Home Secretary for the police and probation service in terms of representation of black and minority ethnic staff. A recent analysis of the ethnic make-up of YOT staff indicated that 8 per cent of YOT managers and 12 per cent of staff were non-white.

A recent Black Regeneration Forum (2000) policy briefing commented on the 'significant, widespread and under-reported' levels of racially motivated harassment and crime, and the resultant fear felt by many residents in deprived areas. In line with others, including the Report of the Stephen Lawrence Inquiry (Macpherson, 1999), this briefing recommended a 'zero tolerance' policy toward racist behaviour, improvements in the reporting and recording of racist incidents, national minimum targets for law enforcement, and Neighbourhood Agreements to prevent antisocial behaviour.

Youth justice

There are, in addition, signs of institutional change within the legal system generally and the youth justice system more particularly. The Crown Prosecution Service announced in August 2001 that thousands of criminal cases were to be reviewed in an unprecedented inquiry into racist and sexist practice, and this could lead to fresh charges against dozens of defendants and thousands of claims for compensation brought by people alleging prejudicial prosecutions. The Lord Chancellor (Irvine, 1999) recently issued guidance to the Judicial Studies Board on how to avoid perceptions of racial bias or insensitivity. In relation to younger people, this quoted a 1994 survey in which only 11 per cent of young blacks and 25 per cent of young whites believed judges gave 'fair and equal treatment to everyone'. As a further example, the Metropolitan Police (2000) issued a booklet on policing diversity which looked at developments one year on from the publication of the Stephen Lawrence Inquiry Report. Among other things, this included guidelines on the use of language and the expression of views that the police force should adopt in relation to people from different communities.

There has also been concern about racism in the prison service, including among young offenders. The Commission for Racial Equality, as a result, announced the launch of a formal investigation into racism at a young offenders' institution and two adult prisons following the murder of a 19-year-old man by a self-confessed racist in November 2000. The CRE predicted that this inquiry would be as far-reaching as the inquiry into the death of Stephen Lawrence and, if evidence of unlawful racial discrimination is revealed, the Commission will be in a position to force the Police Service to comply with a legally binding Non Discrimination Notice requiring action to stop racially discriminatory practices and behaviour.

Summary points

■ Recent statistics suggest that young people from black and minority ethnic groups are overrepresented among young offenders.
■ Crime patterns may, however, be influenced by the age structure and residential location of different ethnic groups.
■ Ethnicity appears to be related to various aspects of the operation of the youth justice system.
■ Initiatives to reduce youth offending include activities with a specific focus on young people from minority ethnic backgrounds.
■ There are recent signs of institutional change within the youth justice system.

14. Provision of Social Services

Although social services cover a wide range of provision, this section focuses on children and young people who are fostered, adopted or in residential care. It examines evidence on the representation of black and minority ethnic group children in these forms of care, looks at the services they receive, discusses the debate over same-race and other placements for children, outlines recent service developments in this broad area, and reports on the extent and efficacy of monitoring by ethnicity.

Numbers and representation

Since information has been collected, the limited available evidence has been consistent in showing how children within the care system are disproportionately drawn from certain ethnic groups: African-Caribbean families and mixed-heritage families (and usually where the birth mother is white) have been typically overrepresented, with Asian children, by contrast, underrepresented (e.g. Bebbington and Miles, 1989; Rowe and others, 1989). In 1991, for example, 19 per cent of children looked after by local authorities were from a minority ethnic background, compared to only 9 per cent of the under-16-year-old population as a whole (Cabinet Office, 2000a). Evidence also suggested that black children in the care system have often entered at an earlier age and remain looked after for a longer period, many with multiple episodes of care.

A survey of local authority adoptions between 1998 and 1999, based on 1,801 children from 145 authorities in England, found similar patterns (Ivaldi, 2000). It showed, for example, that while 90 per cent of adopted children were white, 7.5 per cent were from mixed-heritage backgrounds. Black and mixed-heritage children were also found to be younger than the average on coming into care.

Analysis of Quality Protects Management Action Plans (MAPs) and children and young people from black and minority ethnic group backgrounds confirmed these patterns (Department of Health, 2000d). Findings indicated that more young people than expected from these groups, particularly from dual-heritage backgrounds, were recorded on the child protection register or looked after, and fewer than expected seemed to be receiving preventative family support services. These young people were also more likely to spend greater periods of time looked after since many fostering and adoption units were finding it extremely difficult to recruit Black and Asian carers. The survey was, however, based on incomplete data as many local authorities could not provide information on service take-up by ethnicity. There was a particular lack of information on the numbers and circumstances of mixed-heritage children coming to the attention of local authorities.

> A number of authorities were undertaking detailed audits of services and/or the needs of disabled children and young people from BMEC to provide greater understanding of their needs and develop more appropriate and accessible services.

There is some evidence to suggest that improvements are occurring (Department of Health, 2000i). As part of the MAP evaluations by Social Services Inspectors on children's services during the second year of Quality Protects[12], it emerged that councils were better at reporting the ethnic background of children receiving services than they had been in the previous year. Most could indicate numbers of white, black/ black British, and Asian/Asian British children who received services at the beginning of 2000. About two in three could also provide information on the numbers of mixed race children receiving services. These data meant that some assessment could be made of the proportion of children from different backgrounds who were receiving services. Based on available returns from councils for services in January 2000, it appeared that white and Asian groups were underrepresented in over half the locations and overrepresented in 12 and 4 per cent respectively, mixed race groups were overrepresented in over three-quarters of authorities and hardly ever under-represented, and black groups were overrepresented in over one in three authorities and underrepresented in 7 per cent of locations. It is difficult to draw any firm conclusions from these findings as overrepresentation and underrepresentation may reflect either need or practice factors or some combination of the two.

A clear picture of service use is necessary before priorities for practice development can be determined. The recently established Children in Need Census (Department of Health, 2001a) should be useful in monitoring patterns and trends for this purpose.

---

12 Quality Protects is a national initiative launched by the Department of Health in September 1998. It aims to improve the care and life chances of disadvantaged and vulnerable children by setting national objectives with clear outcomes. Local councils are required to draw up Management Actions Plans to show how they intend to achieve these outcomes.

Local authority social services departments are now required to provide information, including ethnicity based on 2001 Census categories, on all children in need, broken down according to whether they are looked after or supported in families or independently, during one week each year. According to the first sweep of this survey in February 2000, 16 per cent of children in need came from a minority ethnic background. This suggests that these children were between one-and-a-half and two-and-a-half times as likely to be in need as children within the general population. The Children Act Report 2000 (Department of Health, 2001d) pointed to the great overrepresentation of minority groups in London boroughs, and suggested that work with asylum seekers has become a significant proportion of the workload in many of these locations. Future sweeps of the Children in Need census will count asylum-seeking children and families directly.

Services provided by local authorities

Several recent key reports to have assessed and evaluated social services practice for black and minority ethnic groups have pointed to serious shortcomings. These included the Social Services Inspectorate (SSI) report on the inspection of services for minority ethnic children and families (O'Neale, 2000), the 9th Annual Report of the Chief Inspector of Social Services (Social Services Inspectorate, 2000b) 'which draws on the inspection and performance review activity of the SSI to provide an assessment of the current position of social services', and a report from the Family Rights Group (Richards and Ince, 2000) which looked in part at how services had improved over the past two decades since the ADSS/CRE had described them as 'patchy, piecemeal and lacking in strategy'. While all acknowledged aspects of good practice as well as improvements over recent years, they on the whole endorsed the comments of Barn and others (1997) three years earlier that:

> Although there were some positive developments, there is little reason for complacency. The financial hardships faced by local authorities meant that service provision to black families and children remained patchy and incremental.

The recent report from the Family Rights Group (Richards and Ince, 2000) drew on responses to questionnaires completed by 52 local authorities (of the 157 to which they were sent) to investigate how the duty on authorities to provide appropriate services for every looked after child was being met for minority ethnic groups. Generally speaking, a poor service was being provided and there were accusations of neglect by clients from minority ethnic backgrounds. A stark contrast emerged between authorities that did and did not display good practice, and overall:

> Few authorities had accessible services for black families, even failing to offer translated documents and trained interpreters.

Monitoring by ethnicity was also generally non-existent or poorly carried out.

A failing of many services seems to be not knowing how best to provide appropriate services for black and minority ethnic families and, accordingly, a lack of suitable strategies. O'Neale's (2000) report on inspections of services to children and families from minority ethnic backgrounds in eight authorities found that most provision was not sensitive to the needs of these families. Richards and Ince (2000) also commented:

> Many respondents seemed at a loss as to where to start in 'dealing with' Black children and their families. There was acknowledgement that something had to be done but a paralysis regarding how this should be done.

The result may be that professionals intervene to a lesser extent with minority ethnic than other families. Certainly Utting (1997) reported that less preventative work was done with black children and their families to reduce the likelihood that they would enter the care system.

Barn and others (1997) demonstrated concerns about services for children looked after by local authorities by exploring the case histories of 196 black and white children looked after or supported in three authorities, and carrying out interviews with a sample of these. They found significant improvements in social service provision for black children since the Children Act 1989 as well as serious failings. There were, for instance, no written policies on the placement needs of minority ethnic children, a lack of understanding of the requirements of those from mixed-heritage backgrounds, limited training for staff and carers on equal opportunities and anti-racist practice, little evidence of effective monitoring by ethnicity, and poor implementation of anti-racist approaches.

One outcome was a lack of long-term planning that seemed to occur for these children and young people. O'Neale (2000) more recently concluded that assessments were often only partial, that these rarely took account of parenting capacity and the needs of the child and family, and that care planning did not seem to take a lifetime view. Sometimes they did not identify physical and sexual abuse and deal with it as a child protection issue.

The SSI report (O'Neale, 2000) also indicated poor and inconsistent service delivery to black and minority ethnic children and families. Around one in five Year 2 MAPs made no reference to these groups, and in many other cases reference was only limited. A Department of Health (2000g) circular recorded that this is unacceptable.

All councils' MAPs must, therefore, explain for each objective how you are considering and meeting the needs of these groups.

The corollary of a failure to take their special needs into account is that many people from minority ethnic groups feel alienated from and ignored by existing services. A recent Audit Commission (1999) report noted:

Of the people who responded to the Joint Review user and carer survey, less than one half reported that their specific racial, cultural and religious needs had been taken into account. This is a very serious shortfall, although some councils are making very solid progress in remedying it.

O'Neale (2000) is among those to have pointed out how a young person's religion and language are often not recorded on care plans.

Frequently it seems that no special efforts are made to target children and young people from black and minority ethnic backgrounds for the services from which they might benefit. There is widespread concern that, in general, minority ethnic groups have less knowledge than others about service availability (Atkin and Rollings, 1993) and most reports have pointed to a lack of appropriate information, and a shortage of good interpretation and translation facilities, as often in part to blame. An example of an underused service was provided by Butt and Box (1998) who looked at 84 family centres and their use. Although these were appreciated by black families, only a few had specifically targeted such families, used black voluntary organisations to provide information on the services offered, or had specific funding to develop services for this group. Of the 66 centres in England and Wales, 51 did have at least one black worker which seemed to encourage use by black families.

Some research has indicated that rates of service use reflect patterns of referral. Barn and others (1997) reported how Asian families seemed particularly unlikely to refer themselves, suggesting they were less likely to receive 'family support' and more likely to come to notice only when in difficulty. Qureshi and others (2000) carried out a study of South Asian communities in one local authority in order to try to establish the reasons for this limited use of family support services. On the one hand practitioners felt they did not have enough knowledge about the family lives within these communities to offer effective support, and on the other South Asian families were not sure that what was available was relevant to their needs. The importance of specific policies or practice guidelines relating to work with these families was highlighted.

Geographical factors may sometimes be 'blamed' for the lack of necessary services for minority ethnic groups. Although the focus of service need assessment for minority ethnic groups will often be the conurbations in which the majority live, need also arises in areas where members of these groups are present in only small numbers. Low demand from an area may not mean that there is not high need. Many of these issues are applicable to minority groups in rural areas (Henderson and Kaur, 1999). Computer-assisted geo-mapping may be a strategy that authorities need to develop to identify social exclusion existing in quite small geographic pockets.

The recruitment of professional staff is a further issue that has been much discussed in relation to services for black and minority ethnic group young people (Audit Commission, 1999). It has often been argued that many services should be black-led, and this has led to much discussion of monitoring staff by ethnicity as well as training and employment implications (Audit Commission, 1999).

In summary, there are many limitations to the services available to and used by young people from black and minority ethnic backgrounds. In many areas it is the needs of those from dual or mixed-heritage backgrounds that seem most neglected.

Same-race and other placements

Recent years have witnessed recurring debate on same-race versus other placements in fostering and adoption. Historically, the issue stems from the 1960s when white prospective parents could not find white babies to adopt and so turned instead to black babies from residential homes. The prevailing practice then became to place both black and mixed-heritage children with white parents until strong opposition forced a change in policy. This dates back to the inaugural meeting of the Association of Black Social Workers and Allied Professions in 1983 when current practice was vociferously opposed and recruitment of black carers was urged. During the 1980s, a 'same-race' placement policy led to children being removed from white families they had lived with for several years, and it seemed that young black children spent longer in care because there were not enough black families for them to go to. There are, however, no available statistics to indicate the extent to which services differed according to ethnicity.

In more recent years, voluntary organisations such as the British Agencies for Adoption and Fostering, British Association of Social Workers, NFCA and the Commission for Racial Equality have continued to support same-race placements, although they have stressed the need to consider the individual and have argued that a transracial placement may be preferable to a long delay and more time in residential care. The government position has generally been similar. In a circular to local authorities, the Department of Health (1998a) emphasised the need to 'achieve the

right balance' by encouraging ethnic matching where possible but by also making it
clear:

> that it is unacceptable for a child to be denied loving adoptive parents solely on the
> grounds that the child and adopters do not share the same racial or cultural
> background.

It has been stressed that families need to be able to help children placed with them to
appreciate their background and culture, to help them deal with racism and,
particularly for those of mixed origins, understand and take pride in all elements of
their racial heritage. This position had been generally endorsed by the Children Act
1989 as well as by policy guidelines issued from the Social Services Inspectorate
(Utting, 1990). Whilst leaving open the possibility of transracial placement in
exceptional circumstances, these stated that, usually and with all else equal, placing a
child with a family of a similar ethnic origin and religion is most likely to meet his or
her needs. The balance of considerations may vary somewhat for fostering and
adoption where the timescales involved are likely to be different.

Smith and Berridge (1993) summarised the arguments relating to ethnic matching. In
favour, they also cited that black children have to learn from black adults how to deal
with racism, how they need to grow up in black families to develop a healthy identity,
and how all children need to learn about the culture of their family of origin. They
also stressed the need to work in partnership with parents. 'Transracial' family
placement, they suggested, could be better for children than growing up in
institutions, and can result in emotionally healthy children. White families can,
moreover, encourage a child's contact with the black community, and colour, ethnicity
and culture are not necessarily paramount considerations. In line with the prevailing
view, they emphasised that individual needs should be assessed according to the
requirements of the Children Act 1989 before any decision about placement is
reached.

Other research evidence has reached similar conclusions. The British Adoption
Project, an important early study of the adoption of minority ethnic children into
families with two white parents, concluded that white parents could love such children
and that adoption could be successful (Raynor, 1970). In the third sweep of the study,
Gill and Jackson (1983) reported on interviews with 36 children, aged 13 to 15 years,
and their parents from the original 53 families. The authors felt that the findings
generally supported the success of the adoptions. They outlined how the young
people appeared to be doing well at school and getting on with parents and friends,
and although they seemed to 'regard themselves as "white" in all but skin colour',
there was no apparent evidence that a lack of racial pride was associated with low self-

esteem or behaviour problems at the time of the survey. Some of the counter-arguments already outlined were, nonetheless, raised and the authors generally favoured adoption by black parents where possible.

Another longitudinal study has recently been reported by Moffatt and Thoburn (2001). The outcomes of permanent family placement were examined for 254 young people from minority ethnic backgrounds drawn from a cohort of 1,165 British children placed between 1980 and 1985. Successful placements, defined as those not known to have broken down, were not related to the ethnic origin of the child for either adoption or fostering, but linked instead to factors commonly associated with success such as age and absence of problem behaviours. An interesting finding was, however, that boys seemed to do better in 'transracial' than in matched placements, while the reverse was true for girls.

Two other smaller British studies provided some further information on this question. The first, carried out by Tizard (1977), looked at eight children of mixed-heritage within a larger group of children adopted by white parents. The findings suggested that these eight children faced few difficulties, but any more general conclusions are limited by the small size of the sample. The second investigation, reported by Bagley and Young (1979), studied 3 black and 27 mixed-heritage children, with an average age of just over seven years, in 'transracial' adoptions. These authors reached conclusions that might be questioned:

> The children had good levels of adjustment but nearly half the children of mixed parentage saw themselves as White. A fifth of the families had little contact with the Black community and had stereotypical views of Black people.

In summary, there are no reliable data on the longer-term outcomes for black children and young people adopted by white parents and, as the majority of placements these days are with own-race parents, it is also unlikely that there will be any forthcoming evidence in the near future. The issue does, however, remain of some importance, particularly for children from mixed-heritage backgrounds who may regard themselves as black or as white. It is interesting to note, in this context, how many such children and young people brought up in lone-parent households live only with their white mothers.

Developing children's services

Some recent initiatives have sought to develop the services available for children and young people from black and minority ethnic backgrounds. Among these, Quality

Protects (Department of Health, 1999d) is a major government programme to improve the management and delivery of services for children for whom social services have responsibility (looked after children, those in the child protection system, and others 'in need'). This pointed out not only that all its sub-objectives applied to children and families regardless of race or ethnicity, but also included a few that related particularly to these groups and the promotion of greater equity in access to services and outcomes. There is, for instance, a special Department of Health Quality Protects Project Team to develop best practice for minority ethnic children. Among other things, this has the remit to develop inspection standards based on good practice, introduce new data collection procedures to incorporate statistical information on the ethnicity of children from April 2000, and create a new post within the Social Services Inspectorate to ensure that issues of race and culture are taken forward across the children's agenda.

Four demonstration projects have, in addition, been established under the umbrella of Quality Protects (QP) to provide models for local authorities in their work with minority ethnic groups (Singh, 2000). These pilot projects focus on QP objectives and will inform the next Circular. They relate to services for looked after children from dual-heritage families (with a focus on increasing placement choice), Bangladeshi families (focusing on improving educational outcomes), services for Sikh children and families in isolated rural locations (concerning listening to children and the development of the corporate parenting role of councillors) and leaving care support services for African-Caribbean families. Additional projects will also be established.

Also as part of the Quality Protects initiative, the Department of Health (2000a) issued a framework for the assessment of children in need and their families. This provided a systematic way of determining whether a child is in need under the Children Act 1989 and deciding how best to provide help. The Department also published practice guidance for assessing children in need and their families as a companion volume, and included a chapter relating specifically to black children. This offers 'Pointers for Practice' in a wide range of areas from education to identity, and from family history and functioning to racial abuse and harassment.

The consultation on New Guidance for Planning Children's Services (LASSL, 2000) included specific reference to black and minority ethnic communities. It quoted the Report on the Stephen Lawrence Inquiry (Macpherson, 1999), emphasising the need to tackle 'race' issues within the mainstream of modernising programmes if sustainable change is to be achieved. It outlined how improving outcomes for black and minority ethnic children is central, and that:

Services must be planned which aim to bring outcomes for these children to at least the level of the whole community. This will be achieved through services which are culturally sensitive and which recognise and value diversity.

The guidance also stressed the need to involve black and minority ethnic staff and consultants in the process, and to take account of the perceptions of the black and minority ethnic community. It has been superseded by further guidance on coordinated service planning for vulnerable children and young people in England (Department of Health, 2001b) that referred to planning for and with black and minority ethnic communities. As well as stressing the need to tackle 'race' issues within mainstream programmes, it highlighted how black and minority ethnic community groups should be engaged in the planning of services. Children's and Young People's Strategic Partnerships, consisting of 'individuals who together can speak for the community' are recommended to help to improve local services and decide on and implement local community strategies.

Finally it should be recognised that each individual and his or her particular circumstances remain individual whatever the background culture. Often problems and difficulties are complex and result from the interplay of many factors, and those providing services may need additional guidance in these areas. This is illustrated by Farmer and Owen (1995) whose research findings led them to the following conclusion:

Amongst the social workers interviewed there was a laudable absence of attempts to see cultures in terms of fixed characteristics ... but ... in spite of (or perhaps because of) considerable sensitivity in their perceptions, a few workers were somewhat overwhelmed by the number of factors which appeared to be relevant in minority ethnic cases, and they had difficulty in combining them – especially if culture, race and ethnicity were seen not as the total context for intervention but as factors to be added at the end of a lengthening list.

Monitoring by ethnicity

Monitoring by ethnicity has been encouraged in most services for a number of years, but has rarely been carried out with any consistency. In 1992 the Department of Health announced that local authorities were to record ethnic origin, according to 1991 Census categories, for children taken into care and to add a mixed-race parentage category, but this recommendation did not lead to any universal practice. Barn and others (1997) are among those to have pointed to the failure to heed this advice in relation to looked after children. Their research indicated that:

> The mechanisms for monitoring the ethnic composition of staff, service users and target populations varied from reasonable to very poor. Even where such mechanisms existed there was little evidence that they were used effectively.

More generally, both O'Neale (2000) and the Social Services Inspectorate (2000a) outlined the failure of social services to monitor the ethnicity of children and young people receiving services. Among their conclusions, O'Neale (2000) reported 'a lack of clarity around both method and process of collection' although this was less marked for information on staff than on service users. It seemed that service providers did not have a clear idea about what details they should be collecting, who should collect them, when they should be collected, how they should be used and, most fundamentally, why they should be collected. Information on language and religion was particularly poorly recorded. The conclusion of the Social Services Inspectorate (2000a) was much the same:

> Social services are failing to grasp the nettle of ethnic monitoring. Where ethnicity is recorded, this is not always done consistently and there are concerns about classifications being used.

Richards and Ince (2000) did, however, suggest that there was some improvement in the amount of information recorded on the ethnic background of children both receiving services and in the community than had been the case only a year earlier. At the time of their survey, they found that almost all councils could provide data on the ethnic background of young people under 18, and nine in ten could indicate the proportion of white, black/black British, and Asian/Asian British children receiving services at the beginning of the year 2000. About two in three could also provide information on the numbers of mixed-heritage children receiving services. Some authorities and organisations provided excellent models and had a clear idea of why they were monitoring by ethnicity, but on the whole there was a lack of records and monitoring systems and considerable complacency about improving matters. In some cases, the low numbers of black and minority ethnic young people were given as an excuse for not giving this a higher priority.

According to the Children Act 1989, local authorities are required to 'give due consideration to ... the child's religious persuasion'. The Department of Health (2000f) reported some unpublished research undertaken in a city and country authority which found that religion was not routinely recorded. In a 'position statement' update on the collection of ethnic data in central statistical collections (Department of Health, 2001c), the question is raised as to whether it might be appropriate to record religion when measuring service provision and need for certain client groups. The uncertainty about the need to record 'first language if not English' was also mooted.

It is encouraging to note that data on ethnicity will in future be used more consistently to monitor service need. The Department of Health (1999d) identified several performance indicators relating to services for black and minority ethnic children which will be used to help assess whether service objectives are being met. So far three indicators have been proposed. The first is the Children in Need Census introduced in February 2000, which reports on the ethnicity of children in need defined as the proportion of children in need from ethnic minorities divided by the proportion of children in the local population that are from ethnic minorities. The second relates to looked after children and is defined as the proportion of children looked after from ethnic minorities divided by the proportion of children from ethnic minorities in the local authority. The third addresses the concern that minority ethnic children may be disproportionately represented among care leavers who leave school without qualifications, and is the percentage of young people leaving care aged 16 or over with at least one GCSE at grades A* to G or GNVQ. The indicator will first be used in autumn 2000 although an ethnic breakdown is unlikely to be in operation until spring 2002.

Summary points

■ Children and young people from African-Caribbean and mixed-heritage families continue to be overrepresented among the looked after population.

■ Several key reports have pointed to serious shortcomings in social services provision for children and young people from minority ethnic backgrounds.

■ Most young people who are fostered or adopted are placed with families from a similar background. This is in line with current views on best practice.

■ An increasing number of initiatives is being developed to improve social services for young people from black and minority ethnic backgrounds.

■ Although there has been much criticism of the lack of effective monitoring by ethnicity on the part of local authorities, there are some recent signs of improvement.

15. Young Refugees and Asylum Seekers

In recent years the issue of young refugees and asylum seekers has received greater prominence than ever before. In part this is because this population is rapidly growing, particularly the numbers of children arriving in Britain alone, and in part because there are tremendous service implications as the young people concerned face a wide range of problems spanning education, health and social care.

Definitions and status

The problems surrounding the definition of refugees have been stressed (United Nations High Commissioner for Refugees, 1994). Broadly speaking, the term refugee is applied to involuntary migrants who are seeking asylum, or have Exceptional Leave to Remain (ELR) on humanitarian grounds, as well as those who have full refugee status. Technically, however, people applying for refugee status are known as asylum seekers while they are awaiting a decision and are only 'anticipatory' or 'emergency' refugees. Only about 10 per cent of those who apply for asylum in Britain gain refugee status. Fewer than half of the rest are given temporary leave to remain. The remainder are issued, often with little notice, with deportation orders.

Unaccompanied young asylum seekers are children and young people under 18 years who arrive in Britain without a parent or adult carer. A claim for asylum needs to be made before their eighteenth birthday which, if approved, means they become a refugee. If their application is turned down they remain the responsibility of the local authority if they are already so, or they are referred to the National Asylum Support Service (NASS) and they may be relocated elsewhere in the country under the dispersal scheme.

Legislation and guidance

The treatment of young refugees and asylum seekers is directed by international guidance from the European Council on Refugees and Exiles (1996). Their fundamental rights are outlined in the 1981 UN Convention Relating to the Rights of Refugees as well as the Declaration on the Rights of Persons belonging to National or Ethnic, Religious and Linguistic Minorities (UN General Assembly, 1992; Joly and others, 1997). Some of the key pronouncements of the latter declaration are:

> Persons belonging to national or ethnic, religious and linguistic minorities (hereinafter referred to as persons belonging to minorities) have the right to enjoy their own culture, to profess and practise their own religion, and to use their own language, in private and in public, and without interference or any form of discrimination. [Article 2]

> States shall take measures where required to ensure that persons belonging to minorities may exercise fully and effectively all their human rights and fundamental freedoms without any discrimination and in full equality before the law. [Article 4]

> National policies and programmes shall be planned and implemented with due regard for the legitimate interests of persons belonging to minorities. *[Article 5]*

> Everyone has the right to seek and to enjoy in other countries asylum from persecution. [Article 14]

The UN Convention on the Rights of the Child and the Children Act 1989 are also clearly relevant (see pages 134–5).

More recently the Immigration and Asylum Act 1999 has outlined the UK's obligations under international law towards asylum seekers. This legislation is controversial and it has been suggested that children of asylum seekers are especially vulnerable:

> There is a very real danger that the Act will exacerbate the already dire situation that exists for many refugee children. Many will find themselves isolated from their communities, living on low incomes in poor quality accommodation, facing harassment and having difficulty in accessing basic services. Marginalisation, stigmatisation and social exclusion will rise and some children will drift into exploitative and harmful situations. Perhaps this is because the Act makes very few direct references to children and, once again, one can only conclude that refugee children have been perceived as refugees first and children second, rather than vice-versa. (Smith, 2000)

Smith (2000) also pointed out that, although just over half the world's refugees are children, the Act fails to mention the UN Convention on the Rights of the Child and take it fully into account. Concerns include the likelihood that children will receive inadequate safeguards against arrest, search and detention (if, for example, there are doubts about their age or story), whether they will be given enough time to state their case and make appeals, the suitability of the support package that includes vouchers for young people and the impact this may have on their diet, accommodation on a no-choice basis, and possible dispersal to areas that lack appropriate health and social services and which may mean abandoning education, friends and carers.

The numbers involved

The Home Office publishes annual statistics on the numbers of applications for asylum in the UK, but these do not include regional and local rates and provide only limited information on young people. Although better information is available from specific studies of refugees in some areas of London, there is 'very little hard information on the numbers of refugees across London' (The Health of Londoners Project, 1999). The Audit Commission (2000a) has stressed that:

> It is difficult to plan for this group as there is currently no information system/ database that is set up to provide accurate statistics.

Many estimates have, however, been derived. Some relate to children and young people using services. The Refugee Council (1997) suggested there were 46,000 refugee children in Greater London schools in 1997, representing around 80-85 per cent of all school-aged refugees in Britain. Storkey and Bardsley (1999) produced a similar estimate, based on a combination of approaches including some school surveys, Census and other statistics, of around 45,255 refugee children in British schools in 1996/7, 88 per cent of whom were in London.

Social services departments, which have been required since 1997 to record their caseloads of asylum-seeking families with children and unaccompanied children, also demonstrate how the size of the population is rising. The average weekly caseload across London at the beginning of 1999 was approximately 15,000 single adults, 9,000 families and 1,900 unaccompanied children, an almost twofold increase over the previous year (Storkey and Bardsley, 1999). A later report (Jacobson, 2001) suggested that by 2001 these numbers had risen to 19,000 adults, 12,000 families and 4,000 unaccompanied children.

Other information on young asylum seekers confirms the marked increases in numbers over recent years. The Association of London Government (1998) reported, for Greater London as a whole during the week ending 21 August 1998, a total of 7,673 families with children seeking asylum as well as 1,175 unaccompanied children. Kohli (2000) suggested that nearly 4,000 unaccompanied asylum-seeking children came to the UK in 1999.

These figures are within range of Home Office Asylum Statistics UK. According to this source (Woodbridge and others, 2000), a total of 3,349 young unaccompanied asylum seekers aged 17 years or less applied for asylum in the UK during 1999. This figure represented a ten per cent increase on the similar numbers for 1998 and a three-fold rise since 1997. Almost half the young people had come from former Yugoslavia, with Afghanistan, Somalia and China being other main countries of origin.

In response to a question in the House of Commons, Hansard (2000) reported that a total of 2,597 unaccompanied young asylum seekers were accommodated in care homes in the week commencing 2 April 1999 and that the estimated number for the week commencing 31 March 2000 was 5,193. These figures were calculated from returns from local authorities claiming payment of the UASC special grant and indicated that social services departments were supporting more than twice the number of unaccompanied minors as a year earlier.

Services provided by local authorities

Unaccompanied refugee children are covered by either Section 17 or Section 20 of the Children Act 1989. Under Section 17 they may receive little support from social services departments and can be placed in bed and breakfast accommodation. Under Section 20, by contrast, they are regarded as 'looked after' and in theory protected by the same safeguards as other children. They should be fostered or accommodated in a children's home (although in practice some are still placed in bed and breakfast accommodation), and the local authority maintains responsibility for their welfare until at least their eighteenth birthday. These young people will also be eligible for support upon leaving care under the new Children (Leaving Care) Act 2000.

Information on services received by unaccompanied asylum seekers is limited, but what is available highlights this variability in provision. Some relevant evidence is included in the Audit Commission (2000b) report on the implementation of the Asylum and Immigration Act. This indicated that four in five of the over 5,000 young people in the care of local authorities in April 2000 were aged 16 and 17 years, and all were supported by either London boroughs or Kent or West Sussex. The greatest concentrations were found in the boroughs of Hillingdon, Islington and Haringey. The report suggested that many of these young people received a worse service than other children in need, with fewer authorities offering them a full needs assessment, and only one in three authorities having individual care plans in place for all those looked after. It also reported that half these young people over 16 years, and around one in eight of those who were younger, were placed in bed and breakfast or hostel accommodation for single adults. Difficulties were also noted for young people making the transition from care to independence.

Further evidence is provided by a survey carried out by Barnardo's (2000) in March-April 2000 on services provided to unaccompanied asylum-seeking children. A questionnaire was completed by 54 authorities in England, Wales and Scotland on the 2,718 young unaccompanied asylum seekers in their care. Most authorities took responsibility for fewer than 50 young people, but the range in any one locality was from 377 to 1; 71 per cent of these young asylum-seekers were 16 or 17 years old, and 29 per cent were under 16 years.

A variety of practices was identified. Most authorities said they provided services through children's teams or through a combination of children and asylum teams: the former was more likely when young people were regarded as children in need. Foster and residential placements were used in most cases, although other placements were also made. Overall, only 28 per cent of authorities said they had specific policies for unaccompanied children, and 62 per cent said they had not included them in their Quality Protects management action plans (MAPs). The report concluded that:

> One of the main messages evident from the comments is that Authorities recognise that they are experiencing difficulties in delivering services to these young people and many of them are trying to find ways to improve their service provision.

The main problems that arose seemed to include finding enough suitable placements, language problems and lack of access to interpreters, and knowing the age of young people, which reflected the findings of other surveys and reports in this area. Kohli (2000) also highlighted difficulties in day-to-day social work practice, such as communication between young asylum seekers and social workers, and the special problems that arose when care arrangements at home broke down, parents were ill or died, or there was suspicion or evidence of child abuse.

Norton and Cohen (2000) carried out a Greater London study to examine, qualitatively, youth work policy and practice for young refugees. Their aims were to map the main youth work provision, see which agencies were involved, find out what was being done, gain an impression of what young refugees thought about youth work needs and provision, and look at the pros and cons of the present situation to make recommendations for practice and training. An enormous diversity of need was identified among young refugees aged between 8 and 25 years:

> Our overarching recommendation is the development of an appropriate and relevant youth work provision for refugee communities.

These authors stressed the need to work with the local community, and for mainstream provision to provide facilities for young refugees.

It is evident that there is a great need for appropriate service development in this area. Among other things, the Audit Commission (2000a) has, on the basis of its own and others' findings, pointed to the need for an 'urgent review' to specify appropriate forms of care for unaccompanied minors, agree a standard procedure for age determination, and ensure that the grant structure meets the reasonable costs of their support.

Health

Less attention has been paid to the health needs of young refugees and asylum-seekers than to their needs for education and social care. However, as Jacobson (2001) pointed out, refugee health issues overlap with those for minority ethnic groups in general as well as for others suffering the effects of disadvantage and exclusion. (Refugee families with children are, for example, entitled to only 70 per cent of the value of income support paid to other families in the UK.) An additional issue, however, may be a lack of information on their health status. The Department of Health (2000c) noted:

> Unaccompanied refugee children are unlikely to have medical records from their country of origin and any medical history they themselves give is likely to be incomplete. Their immunisation status may be unknown and a course of primary immunisation may need to be undertaken. Children may have had no previous child health surveillance and may well not have undergone neonatal screening for congenital abnormalities or inborn errors of metabolism. Children may suffer from malnutrition and depending on country of origin conditions to consider include tuberculosis, hepatitis B and C, malaria, schistosomiasis and HIV/AIDS.

Many do register with GPs, and the main barriers to using NHS services seem to concern language and cultural differences, attitudes and awareness of NHS professionals, and the availability of information about provision.

The Health of Londoners Project (1999) carried out a detailed examination of the health of refugees but did not have a specific focus on children. Generally speaking, it appeared that there is more concern for the mental than the physical health of these groups, a conclusion also generally reached for young people. Many accounts based on case histories have emphasised the stressful conditions refugee children have often fled, and highlighted the uncertainty they can feel upon arrival in Britain (e.g. Okitikpi and Aymer, 2000). The wide range of problems these children and their families face can mean it is difficult to know how best to work with them. They may be physically ill, separated from their families, and showing symptoms (such as sleeplessness and nightmares) of the trauma they have suffered. They may, in addition, not speak English and have problems communicating properly both because of language barriers and because they do not want to talk about their experiences. Some may want to stay in this country, some may want to go home, and some may be uncertain. Ascertaining their best interests is not always easy.

It has been claimed that the mental health needs and service provision for the growing numbers of refugee children under 18 years have received scant attention. It has also been suggested that serious psychiatric disorder may be present in up to 40 or 50 per cent of young refugees as has been found in studies in the United States (Hodes, 1998). Disorders may arise following migration or if pre-existing conditions have been exacerbated by stressful experiences.

The needs of young refugees in Lambeth, Southwark and Lewisham (Community Health South London, 2000) were examined through consultations with 34 refugee children aged from 12 to 16 years, as well as 211 service providers and policy officers from health, education and social services, and 20 community and youth workers. Over half the young people felt their health had worsened since arriving in Britain, and more than half were critical of the service they had received from their GP, often feeling they were not listened to. Most, except for those with a good understanding of the health service or with English-speaking relatives, had experienced problems accessing services. They thought their health had been negatively affected by their emotional well-being, poverty, poor housing, experiences of bullying or separation from family members, language problems, worry about their families, and loneliness.

Education

In Britain, as in other European countries, most children of refugees and asylum seekers are admitted to school where, if necessary, they are taught English. Local education authorities are legally bound to make this provision for all children of compulsory school age in their locality, and to take account of their age, abilities and special educational needs in so doing. This applies irrespective of a child's immigration status or rights of residence and accordingly includes young asylum seekers.

Extra government support is available for schools providing education for children of asylum seekers dispersed to cluster areas under the Immigration and Asylum Act 1999. This is to assist them to provide English language tuition and to help the pupils settle in quickly. Free school meals and milk are also provided for children of asylum seekers who are themselves in receipt of support under the Act. Local education authorities have discretionary powers to provide assistance with school uniform. Supplementary schools (see pages 51–53) have a clear and potential role in relation to young refugees and asylum seekers.

Several reports have pointed to the special problems young asylum seekers and refugees can have in settling in to school (McDonald, 1995; Rutter, 1995). This is likely to be a new experience or at the very least rather different from the education they received in their homeland. New curricula, different styles of teaching and methods of learning, and quite possibly very different attitudes to discipline, are likely to be encountered.

Peer research on the educational support needs of young refugees and asylum seekers in Kensington and Chelsea confirmed this picture (Abebaw and others, 1998). Interviews with secondary school pupils, as well as local education professionals and adult refugee community groups, suggested that a lack of language skills was one factor making integration more difficult, and that more general language support in and out of the classroom would be welcomed. Difficulties in settling in were exacerbated by the isolation of young people from their families, many of whom were living alone or looked after by the local authority, who often felt lonely and depressed and had few friends. Some felt they were treated badly and were the object of racist behaviour and bullying.

These pupils often reported unmet support needs. While often positive about their schools and teachers, students did seem to want more help, including increased teacher support in the classroom, refugee support workers, peer education, and the necessary information and advice to make informed choices. Most of the young people seemed content with the progress they were making, but a number would have liked more encouragement. Stronger links between schools and refugee groups in the community were called for to provide parents with information on their child's education and involve them more. A need for more community youth provision specifically for refugees, particularly when newly arrived in Britain, was also emphasised.

Similar conclusions were drawn from interviews in five languages with 34 refugee children aged from 14 to 18 years in 1997 (Newham Refugee Centre, 1997). The study looked at the perceptions and awareness of teachers about refugee pupils' experiences and educational performance in Newham, a borough with around 4,500 refugee children in schools. It also looked at the scale and quality of provision supporting these students' needs. One interesting observation from this study concerned the identification of refugee children:

> Most heads and teachers rely on unscientific methods to identify refugee children

by taking account of nationality rather than migration experiences.

Young voices

To complement the literature on young refugees, a series of interviews was carried out specifically for this report by one of the authors (SH) with members of the Somali Youth Project and the Gheez Rite Eritrean Youth Project, as well as young refugees at Hackney College. This section presents illustrative extracts from those interviews.

Some respondents talked about the effects of post-traumatic stress, loss and isolation.

> We were children but we saw things you can't imagine, some of us saw our mothers, our fathers, our brothers or sisters taken away, tortured and killed. We lost our country, our families, homes, futures, everything.

> We have to start from scratch, some people they do try to help but I don't think they can understand, for them it's like a film or something, but if you've been that frightened you know ... some of these people think we come for the easier life, for the houses or the money ... you lose everything and no-one wants you or knows what you carry inside you ... you see those things written on the walls ... and some of the places they send you are so frightening ... away from your own people. Imagine I came from Somalia and then I am in Middlesbrough in winter ... it was so cold and the only person I knew was a relative in London.

Sometimes this specifically involved the fear of officials.

> You hear about war, and all war is terrible, but a civil war is something much worse and you never know who or what you can trust again . . . you know, these people they ask you questions and they say 'Why didn't you tell us the truth?' but we see these people [officials] and think they are going to send us back or put us in prison.

> My mother came to me crying – she saw the soldiers searching in the buildings across the street and she said 'tonight you have to leave'. We walked and walked in the darkness and all the time we listened for the soldiers. We heard shooting and I thought my heart would stop with fear I was so scared. We travelled at night and we got to . . . . I got work as a servant with this . . . family, it was bad, they treated me so badly but I stayed because I knew they travelled and I prayed one day they would come to England. When we came I did not even know which country we were in but I looked up and I recognised that big sign 'Heathrow'. I ran away and I was alone on the streets of London for days, then I saw a man he looked like we do, and I went up to him and he told me where to find my people . . . . You look shocked, you knew us in College and we are different people there, but we have to survive Steve, we have no choices.

Some young people commented on the assumption some people made about how all young refugees are 'the same'.

> People think we are all the same but we are very very different – our cultures, our history, our religion, our languages, everything, maybe even we were enemies back home . . . 'oh you are a refugee, this is for you'. They can put you in places where the people who are fighting you back home are . . . at college we all had to get along but sometimes it causes trouble . . . some places you have to be careful.

> People they shout at you like you're stupid, you don't understand, I could not speak English but I knew when people were shouting at me – you can see it in their faces – you're just another refugee, a nuisance . . . OK we have lost everything and we have to take what help you give – we were so happy when the council gave us the flat even though the estate is not good – but we are still people just like you, not just another refugee, we had a country just like you.

A few told about how they had had to grow up quickly and assume family responsibilities.

My mother she just sits and cries, she is very depressed, I have to do so many things but what about me and my life? I am so sorry for my mum but it's different here ... it's just you, there's no support from the rest of your family and you have to do it all. How can my mother speak to me about things like that – I am her daughter. But she can't speak English. I have to be everything, mother, sister, social worker ... and still do my essays.

Issues of confidentiality were also raised.

Sometimes you know those translators aren't telling them exactly what you said but you haven't got the language to say 'wait a minute' ... and some of these people they aren't trained properly – they don't understand about confidentiality. They are saying one thing to the person and another to you. And they know your community ... a person like that can cause a lot of trouble for you ... You know, if they are from another clan, they ask you 'What is your name?' and you can't trust them.

Effects on schooling and education were often important to these young people.

In school I was so frustrated; back home I had good grades and I knew the work but I could not speak the language. And the teacher thought I was rude – back home if you look in an adult's eye it is disrespect. I look away and the teacher thinks I am being rude. You don't understand, you feel stupid and people are laughing at you and you get into trouble. But at home people say you mustn't follow the kids' example here – you don't know what to learn – who to copy ... I couldn't wait to leave.

And for some it worked out well.

College was better – we had a mixed group of teachers, some from our home, but all of them, I thank God, they gave us unconditional love. The English ones as well. They knew about what we had been through and what we needed. They had faith in us and they knew how to help us or where we had to go to get help. They encouraged us to feel we could succeed here – to go to university.

Some explained how they had been motivated to become involved in setting up their youth or community project.

We set up this project because the young people were losing themselves, losing their culture – they don't feel they belong here – some of them don't even know their home or language or they won't talk about it. Some of them are getting into trouble and their parents or their older brothers and sisters can't cope anymore ...

we had to set something up where they could learn to be proud of their past and get motivated.

We said to ourselves God has spared us and we have to do something for our children, so we went wherever they were – anywhere on the streets, in the park, to the schools and we asked them what do you want? Let us see what we can do for ourselves .... Some of the young people were losing their identity. Getting into trouble on the streets. Some of them were even ashamed to say they were from Somalia. They say they are not ... there is no Somalia anymore.

Our community is so broken up now – we have to help ourselves and our children to be proud of themselves again.

Despite their experiences, there was still optimism.

Things have happened in my life I will never forget – you can't imagine. But I am 100 per cent proud of being a survivor.

Summary points

- The numbers of young refugees and asylum seekers in Britain have increased markedly in recent years. This includes those who arrive in this country unaccompanied by a parent or other responsible adult.
- Most of these young people are placed in London boroughs, Kent and West Sussex.
- The social services support received by unaccompanied refugee children depends on which section of the Children Act 1989 they are covered by.
- Not all authorities have specific policies for unaccompanied children, and most experience difficulties in making provision for these young people.
- On the whole there is more concern for the mental than the physical health of young refugees and asylum seekers.
- There is evidence that these young people face difficulties at school. Extra support, and stronger links between schools and the community, are among their identified needs.

16. The Community Context

Understanding and interpretation of young people's lives, as described in earlier chapters, is enhanced if the community context in which they are set is taken into account. Society and its operation are also relevant to the discussion of children and young people's experiences of racism as outlined in Chapter 17. This chapter accordingly provides some information on this background by looking briefly at Britain's history as a multicultural nation, the contemporary social context as reflected by current discussion, debate and action, surveys of public opinion, messages from the media, and the legal framework.

Britain as a multicultural nation

It is important to acknowledge Britain's long history as a multicultural nation (File and Power, 1981) from the outset. As Fryer (1984) pointed out:

> Black people – by whom I mean Africans and Asians and their descendants – have been living in Britain for close on 500 years. They have been born in Britain since about the year 1505.

Moreover:

> There were Africans in Britain before the English came here. They were soldiers in the Roman imperial army that occupied the southern part of our island for three and a half centuries.

The perception, nonetheless, has often been that Britain, until recently, had been a 'white' country.

> The notion of a multi-cultural Britain denotes ... recognition of the existence of a citizenry composed by people of different colours and celebrating a diversity of cultures. But this has been so for only the last three decades at the very most, and it

is not universally embraced. Until mass migration from the Commonwealth Caribbean, the Indian sub-continent and Africa from 1948, Britain was seen as a white country; indeed, in many parts of Britain and the contemporary world, the country is still seen as 'white people's country', reflecting the image of an exclusive imperial order. (Goulbourne, 1998)

This has been challenged vociferously in latter years when there has been an upsurge of interest in the history of black people in Britain, not least because many young black people born here were seeking to understand more about their roots and to have their presence recognised. The Brent Library Service 'Roots in Britain' exhibition and book (Alexander and Dewjee, 1981) was an example of an initiative developed to combat the general lack of information in this area.

That Britain has had a multi-racial society for at least 400 years is not generally known. The size of the Black community and its record of positive contribution to British society will surprise many. The struggle against the ambiguous status of Black people in Britain today has parallels in the past which should be of particular interest to educators.

Much of the contemporary situation in Britain, in terms of people's attitudes, expectations and feelings, has to be understood within the context of this past. According to Bryan and others (1985):

But for those black pioneers who established our presence here all those years ago, life can have been only an endless struggle against racism. Not simply were they the targets of individual bigots who taunted and attacked them in the streets, they were also up against a whole barrage of racist myths and justifications, expressed through the institutions of the day, designed to exonerate those who profited most from our enslavement . . . . The same myths which were used to justify our subservience as a people in the past have permeated every facet of British culture, and their legacy is alive and kicking.

The contemporary social context

The prevailing views of a society can to some extent be gauged by the content of influential reports and debates and the responses they evoke. The recent Stephen Lawrence Inquiry report (Macpherson, 1999) is undoubtedly the most important document in recent years on race and ethnicity and their impact in the community. Its conclusions have been broadly accepted and seem to sum up the current perspective which, in the words of Macpherson, is that:

> The evidence which I have received, the effect of which I have outlined ... , leaves no doubt in my mind that racial disadvantage is a fact of current British life .... Urgent action is needed if it is not to become an endemic, ineradicable disease threatening the very survival of our society ... racial disadvantage and its nasty associate racial discrimination, have not yet been eliminated; they are as long as they remain, and will continue to be a potent factor of unrest.

Macpherson acknowledged the history of racial discrimination and disadvantage and, referring to the Scarman Report (Scarman, 1982) into the Brixton disorders of 1981, noted that it is 'a sad reflection' on the intervening 20 years that Scarman's concerns remained as relevant in 1999 as they had been in 1981.

One well-reported conclusion drawn by Macpherson was that:

> There must be an unequivocal acceptance of the problem of institutional racism and its nature before it can be addressed, as it needs to be, in full partnership with members of ethnic communities.

This, for the purpose of the Inquiry, consisted of:

> The collective failure of an organisation to provide an appropriate and professional service to people because of their colour, culture, or ethnic origin. It can be seen or detected in processes, attitudes and behaviour which amount to discrimination through unwitting prejudice, ignorance, thoughtlessness and racist stereotyping which disadvantage minority ethnic people. It persists because of the failure of the organisation openly and adequately to recognise and address its existence and causes by policy, example and leadership. Without recognition and action to eliminate such racism it can prevail as part of the ethos or culture of the organisation. It is a corrosive disease.

The problem of institutional racism was not seen as confined to the police services, but rather endemic within the community at large. This was much the message of a Home Office research study (Sibbitt, 1997) which pointed out that whilst perpetrators of violence are relatively few, it is the attitudes of the wider society which sustain them:

> The views held by all kinds of perpetrators towards ethnic minorities are shared by the wider communities to which they belong. Perpetrators see this as legitimising their actions. In turn, the wider community not only spawns such perpetrators, but fails to condemn them and actively reinforces their behaviour. The reciprocal relationship between the two suggests that the views of the 'perpetrator community' also need to be addressed in efforts to reduce racial harassment.

To the extent that hostility, prejudice and fear remain as commonly felt attitudes in the majority population, there is a context in which a minority of that majority may feel tempted to translate their own more extreme versions of these attitudes into action in the form of racial attacks and harassment.

Forces in society change slowly, and a report from the European Commission against Racism and Intolerance (2001) claimed that institutional racism is still systemic in Britain's police forces, politics and media, despite the lessons supposedly learnt from the murder of Stephen Lawrence eight years earlier. The report was particularly critical of attacks on asylum-seekers and migrants coming to Britain and for 'the adoption and enforcement of increasingly restrictive asylum and immigration laws'. It maintained that these policies have contributed to a xenophobic climate in Britain that is negative towards foreigners. It also reported an earlier study by the European Monitoring Centre on Racism and Xenophobia which had claimed that British people were among the most hostile in Europe towards refugees and asylum-seekers and suggested that attitudes had become less rather than more tolerant in the recent past.

The recent Runnymede Trust report on the future of multi-ethnic Britain (Parekh, 2000) is another significant document. This called for 'rethinking the national story and national identity' and stipulated how:

any long-term strategy must involve moving towards a much greater public recognition of difference – the rights of communities to live according to their own conception of the good life, subject to certain moral constraints.

Criticised by some for its claim that the term 'British' has acquired exclusive, racial connotations, the report asserted that the way forward lay in 'building a pluralistic human rights culture':

England, Scotland and Wales are at a turning point in their history. They could become narrow and inward-looking, with rifts between themselves and among their regions and communities, or they could develop as a community of citizens and communities.

It also acknowledged that new communities are often strongly identified with family, cultural and religious traditions of origin, and that:

Since racism has continued, assimilation has come to be seen as an impossible price to pay – blackness and Asianness are non-tradable. Cultural difference has come to matter more.

However, it also pointed out the fluid and complex nature of identity:

> Communities today are neither self-sufficient nor fixed and stable ... many
> individuals with a strong sense of belonging and loyalty towards their communities
> do not intend their personal freedom to be bound in perpetuity by communal
> norms. The rights of communities must be balanced, therefore, against the rights of
> individuals to move away from their community. If necessary, this right must be
> supported by law.

The report, which highlighted a wide range of contemporary themes and concerns,
and did not present a totally harmonious picture of Britain as a multicultural society,
was the result of a two-year think-tank of 23 'distinguished individuals drawn from
many community backgrounds and different walks of life'. It listed among its
conclusions the need to promote racial justice in Britain, to address and eliminate
racism, to improve monitoring by ethnicity, and draws together recommendations in
areas as diverse as: the arts, media and sport; education; employment; government
leadership and structures; health and welfare; immigration and asylum; legislation;
organisational change; policing; and the wider criminal justice system.

Not only documents and debate, but also deeds and actions, provide important
pointers to the social context and prevailing attitudes. The events of summer 2001
involving Asian and white young people in Oldham, Burnley, Bradford and other
northern towns indicated widespread discontent and highlighted a range of issues
which include racism. The Bradford Race Review (Ouseley, 2001), commissioned
before these outbreaks of violence, was carried out to look at the causes of conflict
between and within communities, what could be done to address these causes, and
how better mutual understanding and respect might be promoted. It concluded that
Bradford represented parallel communities living largely separated lives with
underlying suspicions and hostilities:

> At a time when relationships between communities should be improving, we are
> increasingly becoming divided. There are signs that we are fragmenting along
> racial, cultural and faith lines. Rather than an environment where people are
> respectful and show tolerance for difference, attitudes are hardening and
> intolerance is growing.

The Review outlined what it saw as the reasons for the poor race relations in Bradford,
citing: regeneration processes which lead communities and neighbourhoods to bid
against each other for scarce resources; police methods which cause resentment and
perpetuate stereotypes and mythology; the lack of knowledge and understanding of
different cultures, ethnic groups and religions and faiths; racism and racial disadvantage;
and widespread divisions and lack of communication between cultural and ethnic
groups. All these factors led to strong views held by different groups about each other:

The current Bradford scenario is one in which many white people feel that their needs are neglected because they regard the minority ethnic communities as being prioritised for more favourable public assistance .... . Simultaneously, the Asian communities ... argue that they do not receive favourable or equal treatment and that their needs are marginalized by decision-makers and public-service leaders.

These widely held conflicting views are entrenched and endemic. They may differ from the facts and realities. Nevertheless, they remain the views and perceptions of those people that hold them and remain their version of reality.

A prevailing view is that these conditions have created an uneasy peace, and passed for harmonious co-existence, until a flashpoint revealed the harsher reality and resulted in the episodes. Although it is too early to stand back and 'work out' quite what happened, one contemporary analyst (Harris, 2001) also suggested the importance of: a large pool of unemployed, socially excluded young people; considerable numbers of disenchanted white working-class youths who are vulnerable to racist scaremongering; and the emergence of a generation gap between younger Asians and their elders – 'They are born here and are ready to defend their estates'.

The argument is that young Asians and black youths born and raised in Britain are now less prepared than their parents to tolerate the hostility and rejection they encounter from white society. Others dispute the hypothesis that this is something new, arguing that the young people are merely repeating a process of resistance to aggression which their parents and grandparents had engaged in during earlier outbreaks of inter-communal violence, for example the Notting Hill Riots in 1958 and the disturbances in Brixton and elsewhere in 1981.

These issues are difficult to resolve yet understanding the genesis of events is essential if any action is to be taken to promote harmony in the community. Much depends on public opinion, how it is informed, and how it is manifest.

Public opinion

There have been few large-scale surveys of attitudes towards ethnicity, especially among children and young people. An extensive study of colour and citizenship some decades ago (Rose and others, 1969), information provided by the National Surveys of Ethnic Minorities, views gathered through public opinion polls, and other data available from various smaller studies do, however, provide tangential evidence of what the general public really thinks. As Alibhai-Brown (1999) pointed out, these reveal a somewhat 'confused' picture with indications of both greater tolerance and persisting prejudice.

The annual British Social Attitudes survey has, for instance, suggested that social attitudes towards minority ethnic groups in Britain have become more liberal over recent years. Questions included within the British Crime Survey 2000 replicated those asked earlier in this survey and allow patterns of responses to be compared between 1983 and most successive years until 1991, and 2000 (Home Office, 2001a). What people think in the three key areas of racial prejudice, service delivery within the public sector, and the public sector as an employer, will also continue to be monitored in future years.

Asked about racial prejudice in Britain today as compared with five years earlier, and about racial prejudice in Britain in five years time compared with today, respondents appeared more pessimistic in 2000 than almost a decade earlier. Nonetheless, the 1991 figures have some appearance of representing a 'blip' with patterns out of line with those in the previous eight years, and if 2000 is compared with 1990, a very marginal degree of increased optimism is suggested. There was some indication that the greatest optimism was shown by black respondents. The findings overall point to gradual slow change.

Respondents were also asked whether or not they thought that public services treated members of different racial groups similarly. Although most people in each group (white, black and Asian) thought that treatment was similar, a much greater proportion of minority ethnic groups felt they were treated worse than others. Nearly all differences were statistically significant and they were most marked for black and Asian respondents. In relation to the police, for instance, 3.9 per cent of the white respondents, but 21.9 per cent of the Asians and 34.7 per cent of the black group, said they expected to be treated worse than others as members of the public. The Immigration Service, the Prison Service, the Courts and housing in the private sector, were other areas where differences were particularly notable. Expectations about treatment as employees followed a similar pattern. Asian and black groups again anticipated the worst treatment, particularly within the Police Service, the Prison Service, the Civil Service and the private sector.

A similar picture of slowly changing attitudes emerged from a series of Guardian/ICM polls of a representative population group. It appeared, among other things, that people are becoming more tolerant of interracial relationships. A 1998 poll of 1,200 adults over 18 years found that 53 per cent of white people said they 'would not mind' if a close relative married a black or an Asian person and 36 per cent said they 'would mind a little or a lot'; 21 and 73 per cent of white people taking part in a similar survey three years earlier had given these responses. It is interesting in this context to consider findings from the Fourth National Survey of Ethnic Minorities (Modood and others, 1997) in which members of minority ethnic groups were asked similar questions in relation to marriage to a white person. The vast majority of Caribbeans (84 per cent) said they 'would not mind', compared with 68 per cent of those from African-Asian groups, 52 per cent of Indians and Bangladeshis, and 41 per cent of Pakistanis. At the other end of the scale, those saying they 'would mind very much' ranged from 7 per cent of the Caribbeans to 40 per cent of the Pakistani group.

Two other attitude surveys from around the same date also suggested optimism about future race relations (Commission for Racial Equality, 1998b). Based on 1,500 street interviews with people from South Asian, African-Caribbean and white backgrounds, as well as group discussions with 18- to 25- and 25- to 45-year-olds from each group, it emerged that most thought that race relations had improved in the past 20 years and the majority thought they would continue to get better. Nonetheless participants in the discussion groups thought that racism, which had become more subtle than in the past, remained a problem in British society.

An important question, and one to which there is no authoritative answer, is whether or not children and young people have similar attitudes and are demonstrating similar levels of prejudice as their parents. The indications from the reports of bullying and racist behaviour outlined in Chapter 17 below are not totally encouraging. Nor are the findings from one survey suggesting that young people in Britain were less tolerant than their counterparts in other European countries. Although the majority had positive attitudes towards race equality, there was a significant minority who displayed some negativity: 30 per cent of the British sample disagreed with the concept that all races are equal; a similar proportion said they had committed at least one racist act; only slightly fewer suggested they would not marry outside their own ethnic group; and less than half were in favour of immigration. Nonetheless, over half accepted that multiculturalism had enhanced the country (Music TV/Scantel survey, 1997).

Messages from the media

The Home Office report (Sibbitt, 1997), mentioned above, made the point that the politics and media coverage of immigration control influence and help create a sustaining context for racist attitudes. Citing Gordon (1994):

> Equally blameworthy are those in the mass media, especially the tabloid press, and in political life who inflame racist sentiment. Last year, the *Sun*

newspaper carried a story claiming that Camden Council was housing 'penniless immigrant families' in 'dream homes'. Not only did the Council receive a hundred threatening phone calls following this story, but two Asian children living in the street named by the paper were attacked as they played. So too whenever politicians make speeches about tides and waves which threaten to engulf us, to swamp us, you can be sure that attacks will follow close behind.

The media are important in both reflecting and providing images of society. It is accepted that television and the press (as well as the internet, pop music, film and video) have a powerful influence on young people even if the nature of their effects are debated and unclear.

More theoretically, Shanahan (1995) outlined the concept of 'cultivation analysis' which suggests that those who watch television a lot are more likely to view the world as portrayed. The implication regarding minority ethnic groups is:

> If television excludes certain kinds of people from its world, then heavy viewers should be less likely to recognise such people as important members of society.

It was further concluded:

> It may also be that television contributes to some of the social problems related to authoritarianism such as racism and intolerance.

Others, however, claim that such accounts are too simplistic and do not allow for the complexity of factors influencing attitudes. McCarraher (1998), for example, argued that individual predisposition, social conditions, peer groups and changing technologies all have an impact:

> The results of our research suggest a strongly interactive relationship between parents, children and the media, with each element constantly reacting with the other two in the fertile cultures of individual home environments.

Hengst (1997) agreed, stating that factors such as the media, peer groups, the family, school, and neighbourhood all shape the life-worlds of children.

Many commentators have made observations about bias in the media against minority ethnic groups and how stereotypes are presented and reinforced. Some 20 years ago, Cohen and Gardner (1982) looked at the representation of black and Asian people in the media and concluded that:

> Racism is part of the fabric of our history, woven into our Imperial past, and although we have shed our colonies ... we have not succeeded in shedding the

ideologies and attitudes which underpinned our military and economic subjugation of other races and cultures.

Their book reviewed press, radio and TV coverage of race and found low representation of black people in the media and also, where they were represented, characterisations of black people which relied on stereotypes:

A series of stagy, black stereotypes – our youth were made out to be wayward, muggers and murderous with parents absent or unable to cope with them, in a community full of black Mafia type gangsters.

How far have things changed? Attitude surveys carried out in 1998 (Commission for Racial Equality, 1998b) found that some South Asians, and especially African-Caribbeans, participating in discussion groups said they felt members of their ethnic group were still portrayed negatively in television programmes. Younger members of the groups, however, commented on how skilfully some comedy sketches and programmes dealt with race issues with a sense of humour. A proportion of participants in a street survey also felt that ethnic minorities were currently stereotyped in TV soap operas, although others felt that programmes had become much better in recent years. Black respondents were equally divided in their answers, but Asian and white groups were more likely to say there was much less stereotyping than in the past. Some respondents, especially students, emphasised their wish to see more people from minority ethnic groups in 'normal' roles. One teenager noted, for example, how she appreciated a washing-up liquid advertisement with black people.

A new report from the Independent Television Commission (2001) has argued, nonetheless, that advertising on television fails to reflect or recognise the cultural diversity of Britain. The regulatory body for commercial television reports that people from ethnic minorities:

strongly objected to stereotypes which could, even if unintentionally, encourage damaging racist assumptions.

One of the advertisements selected for mention by participants in focus groups involved children playing musical chairs in which their future careers were predicted by their behaviour. Whereas one boy was identified as a future managing director and a girl as a cabin-crew member, all the children from minority ethnic backgrounds remained in the background and were not allocated a career.

Some educational programmes, notably in the United States, have nonetheless sought to promote positive multicultural attitudes among their young audiences. Sesame Street is an example of such a programme. Assessing its outcome, Gunter and McAleer (1990) concluded that such attitudes did develop amongst its viewers although only following sustained viewing for fairly long periods and only gradually over the period of a couple of years. The research by these authors on popular entertainment programmes led them to conclude that children can learn about the characteristics and habits of ethnic groups from these, and their attitudes might be affected accordingly. Their overall conclusion, nonetheless, was that watching TV did not influence these children's racial attitudes. They proposed, however, that cartoons had a more profound effect and that just one could change attitudes in this respect.

In recognition of the possible ways in which the media might influence attitudes, reference to children and ethnicity is included in most media guidelines. The Children's TV Charter, drawn up at the World Summit on Children's Television 1995 (see Buckingham and others, 1999), included the following clauses:

- children should hear, see and express themselves, their culture, their languages and their life experiences through television programmes which affirm their sense of community and place;
- children's programmes should promote an awareness and appreciation of other cultures in parallel with the child's own cultural background.

These principles were adopted in the Broadcasting Standards Commission (1998) codes of Guidance that stated:

> there needs to be sensitivity towards the differences which exist between people from different ethnic backgrounds. There are times when racial or national stereotypes, whether physical or behavioural, may be used without offence in programmes, but their use and likely effect should always be considered carefully in advance.

> Almost invariably, the use of derogatory terms in speaking of men and women from particular ethnic backgrounds and nations gives offence and should be avoided unless the context warrants it. Great distinctions exist between many people within single countries, let alone whole continents, and a broad community of interest or a common identity cannot always be assumed. The presentation of minority groups as an undifferentiated mass, rather than a collection of individuals with limited interests in common, should be discouraged.

The code of practice issued by the Press Complaints Commission (1999) also outlined how:

- press must avoid prejudicial or pejorative references to a person's race, colour, religion, sex or sexual orientation or to any physical or mental illness or disability;
- press must avoid publishing details of a person's race, colour, religion, sexual orientation, physical or mental illness or disability unless these are directly relevant to the story.

Translating such principles into practice, the British Broadcasting Corporation (2000) outlined guidelines for producers stating that:

> People should not be identified purely by their ethnic origin or colour. They have a wide range of other characteristics and colour should be mentioned only when relevant. 'Ask yourself each time: would you say 'white' in similar circumstances?

Their guidelines on terminology are that:

- 'ethnic minority' should not be a universal shorthand for black;
- geographic or ethnic origin is often more important than colour of skin;
- black should not normally be used to include Asians;
- many people of African and Caribbean origin prefer to be called Black British;
- use black people rather than blacks;
- ask people how they describe themselves.

It is apparent that the media both portray and promote current views of the minority ethnic population and the relationships between groups. It has been suggested, for example, that they contribute to creating panics about crime among young black men through the way that incidents are reported (Mason, 2000). This is an extremely complicated issue on which to collect authoritative evidence, but it is clear that it is one that deserves attention on account of the potential influence that the press, television and other forms of the media have on the prevailing climate of race relations.

The legal framework

A large number of laws and statutes govern the treatment of minority ethnic groups, including children and young people, in this country. Fundamental among these is the Race Relations Act 1976 which set out to outlaw racial discrimination and promote equal opportunities. It has, however, been subject to serious criticism, and the Commission for Racial Equality (1985; 1992; 1998a) has repeatedly indicated that it has not led to widespread adoption of good equal-opportunity practice and has continued to mean that discrimination has had to be challenged through the courts and tribunals. The Race Relations (Amendment) Act 2000 aims to counteract these limitations by strengthening and extending the remit of the Act to combat institutional racism. In particular, it places a new, enforceable positive duty on public authorities, from police to schools and hospitals, to promote race equality, and makes it unlawful for a public authority to discriminate directly against a person, or victimise a person, on the grounds of race, colour, nationality (including citizenship), or ethnic or national origin. The duty to promote race equality involves:

- a general duty on public authorities to work towards the elimination of unlawful discrimination and promote equality of opportunity and good relations between people of different racial groups;
- specific duties to be imposed on some or all of the public authorities to help their performances under the general duty, which will be enforced by the Commission for Racial Equality (CRE);
- CRE codes of practice to provide practical guidance to public authorities on how to fulfil their general and specific duties.

Although the new general duty on public bodies to promote race equality came into force in April 2001, the Act will not become fully operative until May 2002. It therefore remains to be seen how far it will affect race discrimination in such areas as jobs, training, housing, education and the provision of facilities and services.

Also important was the British Nationality Act 1981, which replaced all earlier nationality laws and influenced the status of people entering Britain from elsewhere. It replaced citizenship of the United Kingdom and Colonies with three separate kinds of citizenship: British citizenship, for people 'closely connected' with the United Kingdom, the Channel Islands and the Isle of Man; British Dependent Territories citizenship, for people connected with the dependencies; British Overseas citizenship, for those citizens of the United Kingdom and Colonies who do not have these connections with either the United Kingdom or the dependencies. People became full British citizens only if they were citizens of the United Kingdom and Colonies on 31 December 1982 and had the 'right of abode', i.e. they could live in, leave and re-enter the United Kingdom freely under the Immigration Act 1971.

This legislation has been widely criticised as flouting 'many of the just and fair principles upon which nationality should be based':

> the development of the law on immigration and nationality from 1948 to 1971 followed a continuous line, gradually separating persons supposed to be closely connected with the UK from persons who were British but lacked such a connection. (Dummett and Martin, 1982)

It restricted the numbers who came and settled in Britain, but did so in a way that many felt discriminated against black people who might historically have acquired the right and aspiration to come and settle in the 'Motherland' as a consequence of Britain's imperial and colonial past. The so called 'grandparent rule', extending full citizenship to those who could prove that one of their parents or grandparents was born in the UK, was seen as a way of closing the door to black migrants from the new commonwealth countries, whilst leaving it open to white people from places such as Rhodesia/Zimbabwe and South Africa.

> This meant, in concrete terms, that immigrants from the Commonwealth countries, though remaining British subjects under British nationality law, would be debarred from entering (and settling in) Britain, except as and when required by the British economy. (Sivanandan, 1983)

One of the implications of this legislation at the time was to encourage the families of the migrant minority ethnic population to come to Britain while there was still an opportunity.

Two developments in 1989 were very important for the rights of children and young people, whether of resident, 'immigrant' or refugee status. The first was the Children Act 1989[13] which outlined how local authorities should give due consideration to 'the child's religious persuasion, racial origin and cultural and linguistic background' in making any decision with respect to a child whom they are looking after, or proposing to look after. A similar duty is imposed on voluntary organisations and on the person responsible for the home where a child is accommodated, and on day-care providers. While welcoming the legislation, MacDonald (1991) pointed out that similar requirements did not apply throughout all sections of the Act:

> It is perhaps regrettable that the court's duty to make the welfare of the child its paramount consideration is not accompanied by a specific requirement to include race, religion, culture and language in its deliberations (Section 1). This duty is only laid on local authorities and others providing day care or accommodation for children, at which point they must give these issues due consideration (Section (5) (c), Section 61 (3) (c), Section 64 (3) (c), Section 74 (6). This has opened up the possibilities for different interpretations of what are 'due' considerations as opposed to what are 'paramount' considerations.

However, overall she considered that:

---

13 The Children (Scotland) Act 1995, and the Children (NI) Order 1995, later also indicated that decisions relating to children must take race, culture, language and religion into account.

> The Children Act 1989 provides an exciting and challenging opportunity to reform child care work and radicalise child protection work with black children and their families. Potential for maximising positive use of the Act in enhancing anti-racist social work should not be under-estimated.

Five years later Barn and others (1997) concluded that the legislation had led to significant improvements in social service provision for black children and families, but that there was also a clear need for further achievement.

The second important development in 1989 was the United Nations Convention on the Rights of the Child which included the following relevant articles:

> The right of refugee and asylum-seeking children to appropriate protection and assistance in the pursuit of the rights in the Convention. [Article 22]

> The right of minority groups to enjoy their own culture, language and religion. [Article 30]

> The duty of the Government to take measures to ensure that child victims of armed conflict, torture, neglect or exploitation receive treatment for recovery and social integration. [Article 39]

The broader European Convention on Human Rights is also potentially important, particularly since its implications were strengthened by the introduction of the Human Rights Act 1998.

The European Parliament has adopted further resolutions in this area that endorse the principles outlined in law. Article 13 of the Treaty establishing the European Community, for example, outlined powers to take action to combat discrimination on the basis of sex, racial or ethnic origin, religion or belief, disability, and age or sexual orientation. Subsequent measures have strengthened these powers in areas such as the labour market. Most recently, the introduction of a new directive, to come into effect in July 2003, reinforces the principle of equal treatment between persons irrespective of racial or ethnic origin. This will put new obligations on member states to take a range of measures to promote equal treatment.

At a national level, the Local Government Act 1966 also has relevance to children and young people from minority ethnic backgrounds. This made money available to local authorities to fund additional support for 'immigrant children from Commonwealth countries' and was a response to the arrival of a large number of Ugandan Asians with British passports. This became known as Section 11 funding and was administered through local education authorities either to schools or to fund language support teachers to work with schools. In 1992 the criteria for funding became tighter and were related to meeting targets such as the percentage of pupils progressing through stages of English fluency. From 1996 Local Education Authorities (LEAs) were allowed to use the funding for all minority ethnic children, not just those from the Commonwealth. In 1999, Section 11 funding was replaced by a new grant, the Ethnic Minority Achievement Grant (EMAG), most of which is paid directly to schools to use to raise the attainment of minority ethnic pupils.

Critics of the new arrangement have argued, among other things, that headteachers are not always well placed to make the best decisions about targets, priorities and strategies, and that funding on an annual basis makes it difficult to retain staff and develop long-term plans. Moreover, the only accountability in terms of how EMAG funding is used is through Ofsted inspections. It remains to be seen whether the funding appears effective in raising the attainments of pupils from minority ethnic groups.

Summary points

- Britain has a long history as a multicultural nation.
- The contemporary social context includes serious incidents involving young people from different ethnic backgrounds. Important debate on race and ethnicity can follow, such as in the Stephen Lawrence Inquiry Report and the Bradford Race Review.
- Surveys of public opinion suggest that Britain is gradually becoming more tolerant of ethnic diversity.
- The media play an important role in both portraying and promoting current views of Britain as a multicultural society.
- Legislation governs many aspects of equal opportunities and human rights for all. The Race Relations (Amendment) Act is likely to be the most significant piece of recent legislation in this area.

17. Children, Young People and Racism

Ethnicity relations are a central issue in the study of Britain as a multicultural society. They reflect the way members of different groups think and feel about each other, how they interact, and how their behaviours, deliberate or otherwise, affect others in the community. Prejudice, discrimination, inequality of opportunity and racism (Macpherson, 1999) are their negative manifestations against which it has been necessary to introduce legislation, including the recent Race Relations (Amendment) Act 2000.

It is the delicate nature of ethnicity relations that has, too, been accountable for the complexities and uncertainties surrounding the terminology used to describe people from differing backgrounds. If an unequal status is to be conferred upon those of different origins, then it is understandable if there is considerable sensitivity about how people portray themselves and others. Ethnicity relations also influence expectations and are therefore held partly responsible for many of the day-to-day experiences of young people from diverse backgrounds. The difficulties some black boys, especially those from African-Caribbean backgrounds, encounter at school have, for example, been interpreted as a clash of cultural definitions of behaviour and discipline between teachers and pupils. How services are provided and taken up further reflects expectations about what is needed and what is suitable for whom.

In these and many other ways ethnicity relations intervene in the tapestry of daily discourse. How people see themselves, as well as how they think others see them, can have an impact on their attitudes and behaviour. These in turn affect the representation of ethnicity in the media and society in general, and the cycle continues. Language and communication are important in this context, as are racial and cultural mores and beliefs, and so too is the visibility of skin colour.

The remainder of this chapter addresses just a few of the many issues that arise for children and young people in this context. These are children's experiences of racist behaviour, the characteristics of perpetrators, and how racism might be challenged. First, however, there is a brief section looking at what racism might mean.

What is racism?

Describing racism is no easy matter. Rex (1970), in a seminal work on race relations, defined a race relations situation in terms of three necessary elements:

- a situation of differentiation, inequality and pluralism as between groups;
- the possibility of clearly distinguishing between such groups by their physical appearance, their culture or occasionally merely by their ancestry; and
- the justification and explanation of this discrimination in terms of some kind of implicit or explicit theory, frequently but not always of a biological kind.

A decade or so later Rex (1983) maintained that:

- it was a necessary but not sufficient condition of a race relations situation that there should be a situation of severe competition, exploitation, coercion or repression;
- this situation should occur between groups rather than individuals, with only limited possibilities of mobility from one group to the other; and
- the intergroup structure so produced should be rationalised at the ideological level by means of a deterministic theory of human attributes, of which the most important type historically had been based upon biological and genetic theory.

Nonetheless, as Rex pointed out, such definitions remain open to discussion.

More practically, Smaje (1995) suggested three forms of racism that can affect service delivery:

- where a client is treated less favourably on account of his/her race or colour;
- when services are offered on the faulty premise that equality of care will be the consequence of providing the same services for everyone; and
- if service providers make incorrect assumptions about their clients' needs, either because they fail to take account of the minority ethnic perspective or because they interpret it wrongly.

Smaje concluded that black and minority ethnic children and families accordingly often have difficulty accessing appropriate services.

Gillborn and Youdell (2000) took the argument further in stressing that racism is best identified through its effects rather than its intentions:

> Any set of practices and beliefs that systematically disadvantage members of one or more minority ethnic group can be defined as racist. This approach allows social science finally to catch up to the pervasive and complex forms that racism can take.

Furthermore, racism is not always overt and obvious. As one nine-year-old these authors spoke to explained about her school:

> It's not blatantly here. I mean, you can't, you wouldn't be able to just walk in the school and say 'Oh the school's racist'. You have to take time before you know that.

Even with definitions and descriptions, racist behaviour can remain difficult to identify. It may be expressed in exclusion, discrimination, prejudice, stereotyping, violence and harassment, or some other form, and it may be overt or hidden. It may also be intentional or, as with institutional racism, inherent in the operation of an organisation or service. There has indeed been increasing recognition of 'institutional racism', and its impact on young people, since the Stephen Lawrence Inquiry Report (Macpherson, 1999). It may, for instance, operate in schools:

> educational institutions may systematically treat or tend to treat pupils and students differently in respect of race, ethnicity or religion. The differential treatment lies within an institution's ethos and organisation rather than in the attitudes, beliefs and intentions of individual members of staff. (Richardson and Wood, 1999)

Measuring racist behaviour is, accordingly, fraught with difficulty. Incidents may fail to be recognised on the one hand, while instances of behaviours may misguidedly be referred to as racist on the other. Crime reports which, until 1995, automatically labelled an incident as 'racial' if both white and black people were involved, are an example of the latter. More recently it has been accepted that a standard definition of 'racial motivation', adopted by all police forces in England and Wales, is necessary. This is:

> any incident in which it appears to the reporting or investigating officer that the complaint involves an element of racial motivation; or any incident which includes an allegation of racial motivation made by the person. (Home Office, 1997)

Such a definition does not, of course, remove all controversy surrounding the classification of incidents. Although conclusions may nowadays be more cautiously drawn, there is still debate over what is and is not racist. One of Macpherson's (1999) controversial recommendations was indeed that attacks should be regarded as racist if perceived as such by their victims.

Children's experiences of racist behaviour

Despite limited and patchy knowledge about racist behaviour and its effects on children and young people (Barter, 1999), it seems that many members of minority ethnic groups do experience racism and racial bullying in their everyday lives. Name-calling is most common, but violence also exists. Bullying seems particularly likely in areas with few minority ethnic children.

A number of studies have looked at racist behaviour at school, and a wide range of findings has been reported. Troyna and Hatcher (1992) suggested that:

> race, and racism, are significant features of the cultures of children in predominantly white primary schools

while the Black Child Report 1999-2000 (Peoplescience Intelligence Unit, 2000) indicated that racism affected only a minority of pupils on a regular basis. Of a sample of around 600 young people aged between 11 and 16 years, only 14 per cent said they had been subjected to racism by a peer during the previous four weeks, and a similar proportion reported experiencing racism from a teacher over this same period.

It is likely that the extent of racist bullying varies by school, and an ESRC study of over 2,000 children aged from 6 to 9 years indicated that bullying seemed more habitual in certain schools including those with a higher ethnic mix (Wolke, 1999). A large-scale investigation in Sheffield (Smith and Sharp, 1994) found that racist abuse accounted for only a minority of episodes of bullying (14.8 per cent in junior/middle schools and 9.4 per cent in secondary schools), but this is unsurprising as only a minority of pupils at the schools in question were from minority ethnic backgrounds.

It has been indicated that Asian students are particularly likely to suffer racial harassment in schools, usually in the form of verbal attacks, at both primary and secondary levels (Gillborn, 1990; 1995). A recent study focusing on these groups confirmed high rates but was not able to compare these with rates for children from other backgrounds. Eslea and Mukhtar (2000) gave a questionnaire to 243 Hindu, Indian Muslim and Pakistani 12- to 15-year-olds attending temples and mosques in the Preston and Bolton area of Lancashire. There were no apparent differences between the three groups, and overall 57 per cent of the boys and 43 per cent of the girls said they had been bullied during the current school term. Bullying was not, however, necessarily across racial groups and was as likely to occur between members of the three different Asian group as between Asian and white children.

Another recent study (Connolly, 1998) carried out unstructured interviews with small groups of five- and six-year-olds, and independently observed their behaviour, in a multi-ethnic inner-city primary school. The research interests were social relations, racism and gender identity, and:

> understanding the complex ways in which racism intervenes in young children's lives and comes to shape their gender identities.

Connolly (1998) concluded that:

> while these processes are clearly evident among the young children's peer group cultures, they only can be fully understood by tracing their origins to the social organisation of the school and the local community.

From a different methodological perspective, a ChildLine (1996) study revealed that:

> blatant, unrelenting, openly racist harassment and bullying plays a large part in the daily experience of many black and ethnic minority children at our schools and in the streets.

These conclusions were based on calls for the year up to the end of March 1995 from young people identifying themselves as belonging to a minority ethnic group and/or from children describing problems of racism, prejudice or 'cultural' issues. A total of 1,616 caller records were examined for the study. These included 169 young callers who cited racism, prejudice or cultural or religious difficulties as their main problem, a further 551 young people who said these factors were additional problems, and 138 callers to the Bullying Lines who highlighted racist bullying. Another 758 callers identifying themselves as members of a minority ethnic group were also included.

Although only about 80 callers said that racism was their main problem, ChildLine staff taking the calls indicated that they could 'securely identify 430 children and young people suffering from racist bullying'. In 247 cases, young people mentioned how their relationships (usually adolescent love relationships) were unacceptable to their families because of race, culture or religion. In some cases, they were expected to await an arranged marriage. It is interesting to note that:

> approximately half the callers were explicitly describing their families as racist.

The study suggested:

> there is a generation gap in attitudes, and that whether adults want it or not, many young people are making and will make relationships across cultural, religious and race frontiers. Though most youngsters may be content to make friendships within their own community, others are not.

Tizard and Phoenix (1993) also described how racism could be encountered within one's own family. About half the young people in their sample, who came from mixed-heritage backgrounds but lived in predominantly white families, suggested that either a parent, or a brother or sister, was to some extent racially prejudiced.

One British study examined racist behaviour from the point of view of the victims (Chahal and Julienne, 1999). In-depth interviews with 42 people, as well as focus-group discussions, examined what it felt like to be the target of racist behaviour and what happened in the longer term. The study also asked who was told about the incidents, and the strategies respondents adopted to counter victimisation. The main focus was on adults living in predominantly white areas.

A range of incidents was reported, the most typical of which were racial abuse, intimidation and things being thrown at property. Homes were often the target of attacks, and graffiti, vandalism and objects posted through letterboxes were common. Although adults may have been the target of abuse, children and young people were also clearly affected.

> A harrowing common experience for those with children was the fear and experience of racism when the children were going to and coming back from school . . . . Children were perhaps the most affected because they were not allowed to play outside and in some cases were having problems at their school as well.

It seemed that many incidents were not reported to the police, for a variety of reasons, but that these had a tremendous impact on families as a whole.

Evidence from the 1996 sweep of the British Crime Survey showed that members of minority ethnic groups were more afraid of crime and racial attack than white people, that they felt unsafe both at home and going out, and that they often avoided events and activities (such as football matches, nightclubs and pubs) as a result. This source also indicated that over half of racially motivated incidents, including crimes not reported to the police, were perpetrated by young people under 24 years (Percy, 1998). These findings both reflect and have strong implications for ethnicity relations in the community.

Since 1991, and in relation to even more severe crimes, the Institute of Race Relations has been documenting police responses and convictions following murders with a racial element. According to their analysis (Institute of Race Relations, 2001b) there were, including Stephen Lawrence, at least seven cases in which young men aged less than 20 years had died under these circumstances during the nine years up to the beginning of 2000. Nonetheless, as already indicated, there can be problems in determining whether or not attacks and violence are 'racist'.

In summary, there is considerable evidence of racist behaviour in the community but yet no clear picture about how, in general, children from different backgrounds get on together. A study of school pupils in Lewisham, a highly multi-ethnic London borough, found that 65 per cent of black pupils, 60 per cent of the white group, and 55 per cent of the Asians thought that children from the three different backgrounds get on well together (Franklin and Madge, 2000), which also suggests that a sizeable proportion believed there were problems. Understanding more about ethnicity relations in this sense would seem a crucial area for further study.

Perpetrators of racist behaviour

A key to understanding more about ethnicity relations may be knowing more about the perpetrators of racist behaviour. Sibbitt (1997) collected qualitative evidence from two London boroughs in an attempt to identify those responsible for racial harassment and racial violence such as verbal abuse, threats and other intimidatory behaviour such as vandalism and theft, assaults and indirect assaults (throwing things at people).

Two types of factor seemed to contribute to this racist behaviour, those reflecting stress, delinquency or criminality, and those signalling racial prejudice. Sibbitt (1997) described how a racist career could develop over childhood and adolescence. He suggested that the low-achieving and bullying 4- to 10-year-old, who had grown up in a climate of verbal abuse towards black and minority ethnic groups, might begin by refusing to cooperate with children from these backgrounds at school. By 11–14 years, his (or her) behaviour had probably escalated to become more overtly abusive, threatening and violent and, by 15–18 years, was extremely antisocial and very violent. As perpetrators generally held much the same views as others in the community, their actions became legitimised and encouraged. People of all ages and both sexes became involved, and groups of friends, or families, often acted together.

It is clear that there is inadequate knowledge of how to identify likely perpetrators in order to intervene to try to prevent their racist behaviour. This would seem to be an area in which more research and action programmes should be called for.

Challenging racism

There is also very limited understanding of how best to counter racially motivated behaviour, once detected. Considerable thought, debate and initiative has been directed towards the issue of racism in its many forms and how it can be challenged and overcome, but answers and demonstrated effectiveness of strategies have been much fewer and further between. It is beyond the scope of this report to provide an account of why this is so, although some general observations may be relevant.

First, it is likely that challenging racism effectively depends on a comprehensive knowledge of how such behaviour has developed. Much has been written in this area, and it is acknowledged that the models presented by friends, family and the community, the things young people see and the things they hear, the messages they glean from television, books, magazines, newspapers, films, pop music and other sources, the topics they learn to discuss or keep quiet about, and many other influences all have a part to play. There is rarely likely to be 'just one thing' that leads to racist behaviour. The corollary is that there is no likely single solution. Legislation, service developments, controls on the media, increasing understanding of ethnic diversity, providing appropriate role models, monitoring what goes on, and perhaps adopting a policy of zero tolerance towards racism, are but some of the strategies that have been called for.

Second, it is acknowledged that only a multifaceted approach that impinges on attitudes and behaviours, but at the same time deals with inequality and inequity, has any chance of effectiveness. Nonetheless, as Sivanandan (quoted by Institute of Race Relations, 2001a) wrote:

> In effect there are two racisms in Britain today . . . the racism that discriminates and the racism that kills. The solution to the one is no solution to the other.

As he also pointed out, it is much harder to challenge the racism that leads to unrest and open hostility than the racism that incurs inequality of status and access to society and its provisions.

In practice strategies to address racism are inevitably somewhat piecemeal. Many overarching activities, from changing the law to advocating good practice, have been outlined throughout this report. At a more local level, there is much going on with small groups in varied settings. Working with young children during the early years to promote race equality and help children unlearn racially prejudiced attitudes and behaviours (EYTARN, 1996; Malik, 1998; Lane, 1999) is one example. Increasing understanding between diverse groups in society is another. This is manifest in the forthcoming introduction of Citizenship studies into the National Curriculum and is encapsulated in the recommendations of the recent Bradford Race Review (Ouseley, 2001). This review identified the key issues for young people as:

- limited or non-existent interaction between schools and different communities along racial, ethnic and religious lines;
- open racial conflict and harassment in and around schools;
- failure of schools to recognise and deal with racial incidents;
- lack of curriculum content to promote understanding of different cultures;
- poor levels of school attainment; and
- a shortage of adequate recreational and leisure pursuits for young people who then become bored and engage in antisocial and criminal behaviour.

Recommendations accordingly included the need for early-years education to ensure the development of positive attitudes towards 'diversity, differences and cultures', education for parents to help them to challenge negativity, listening schools to take more account of what pupils and parents think and say, and much more 'positive marketing' of multicultural communities.

Quite how goals such as these are to be achieved is less evident. Bhavnani (2001) recently examined interventions in racism and reached the following rather pessimistic conclusion in relation to training to change attitudes and behaviours:

> Since the early 1980s, millions of pounds have been spent on training to combat racism. Yet it is clear from the present analysis that the training has failed. It has failed because, all too often, its content and approach has been developed in isolation from an understanding of racism in British society as a whole.

Her belief was that:

> there must be a new approach in education and training on combating racism. One that accepts that racism takes on different forms, operates in different contexts and that organisations may reproduce racism through their own distinct discourse. The old approach of off-the-shelf generic racism awareness training may be a thing of the past, or ought to be.

Lane (1999) has added:

> There are no magic ways of countering racism and many people may feel disheartened by trying to do it and not getting very far.

These are challenges that should not be ignored.

Summary points

- Ethnicity relations are central to the issues confronting Britain as a multicultural society.
- Racism is difficult to define, and racist behaviour is not always easy to identify.
- There are indications that many children and young people experience racism and racial bullying on a daily basis, but no clear evidence on the full extent of this.
- There is also little clear information on how children and young people from different backgrounds actually get on together and what they think of each other.
- Developing effective strategies against racism is a major challenge for the future.

18. The Way Forward

The task of this report has been to try to understand the different experiences of young people growing up in Britain, and to identify the differences that matter. There has been a particular focus on the circumstances of those from black and Asian backgrounds, on how young lives vary within these groups, and on how they compare with the young lives of the white majority group. The overall aim of the report is to bring together evidence to provide a basis for deliberations on what society should do to promote multiculturalism in its widest sense and move forward.

Generalisations are not easy to draw. There is clear evidence of disproportionate disadvantage for black and minority ethnic children and young people as a group, but yet a striking impression of diversity both within and between groups. Mixed conclusions are also suggested in relation to the policy and practice that has developed for young people within a culturally diverse society. On the one hand there are countless examples of provision that has been carefully planned and developed, and which seems to work well, but on the other there are significant gaps and omissions and indisputable evidence of need that is not being provided for or met.

There are grounds for both optimism and pessimism on the future of ethnicity relations too. While there is evidence that attitudes between groups are gradually becoming more positive over time, it is still clear that racism continues to exist in a wide variety of forms.

The meaning of ethnicity within the community is changing all the time. The size of the black and minority ethnic population in Britain has risen significantly over recent years (children and young people from these groups now represent over one in ten of those in their age group) and will continue to increase over the next decades. At the same time, the divisions between minority ethnic groups are becoming less clear. The marked increase in inter-racial unions has produced large numbers of children and young people of dual or mixed heritage. The diversity among young people in contemporary Britain is becoming ever greater.

The issues at stake do not necessarily remain static either. Although the underattainment, on average, of some minority groups at school, the disproportionate numbers of young people from black and minority ethnic groups who are looked after by local authorities, youth justice issues, the unmet health needs of black and minority ethnic groups, problems of racism and discrimination, and the capability of services to meet the needs of these groups, continue to retain current priority, their interpretation and how they might be addressed have changed considerably over time. The vast majority of these young people today are full British citizens born and brought up in Britain by parents who are likely also to have spent their entire lives in this country. They are fluent in English, often have a lifestyle that differs little from young people more generally, are British and to differing degrees feel British.

Furthermore, even where an underlying concern remains similar, the presentation of a problem may vary. Current explanations for disproportionate numbers of pupils from some black and minority ethnic groups being excluded from school, for example, parallel the reasons given by Coard (1971) on how the West Indian child was made 'educationally subnormal' in the British school system. Recent political exchanges about 'floods' of asylum seekers is, furthermore, a revisiting of the immigration issue that arises from time to time. The groups singled out for attention may change but the underlying theses of prejudice, hostility, disadvantage and rejection endure. As Joly and others (1997) stated:

> Many characteristics formerly attributed to immigrants to Europe are now attributed to refugees. Many of the themes of ethnicity, belonging, nationality and xenophobia are now being increasingly debated in the arena of refugees, rather than in relation to immigrants. With immigration channels largely closed, refugees have become the new target.

It is difficult to know where to start in drawing conclusions for the way forward. There are so many issues to be addressed, but yet no blueprint of what might be done. Sometimes it is information which is lacking, sometimes resources, and sometimes motivation. Recommendations for action in specific areas have been outlined throughout this report. What follows is a brief discussion of six areas in which energies might be directed in an attempt to tackle just some of the main priorities for children and young people from diverse backgrounds in Britain today. These are:

- making sure we have informed and balanced evidence on the issues of concern so that we really know what is happening;
- developing and promoting policy and practice that can and do meet the needs of all children and young people in Britain today;

- encouraging the appropriate monitoring by ethnicity and adoption of performance indicators;
- doing what we can to promote intercultural harmony and reduce racism;
- getting the messages right and getting them across; and
- listening to young people themselves.

Informed and balanced evidence

One of the clear messages from this review is the need for better knowledge about black and minority ethnic groups in Britain. Only with such understanding are we able to document differences, ascertain the circumstances in which these do and do not occur, identify risk and protective factors, and establish whether or not there is unmet need or inappropriate practice. High-quality research is an important tool in achieving these goals.

The evidence presented in the literature and reviewed in this report is drawn from studies employing a wide range of methodologies with samples of various sizes and composition, varying degrees of representativeness of the population as a whole, differing time scales, contrasting definitions of ethnicity, and varying types of analysis and interpretation. Painting a composite picture from the sum of all its parts is no easy matter.

Research findings have, nonetheless, contributed significantly to what we know and to an understanding of what we do not know. They have clarified some of the priorities that exist for future investigations in this area and highlighted that knowledge will advance only if strict methodological criteria are observed. Among other things, it seems important that there is a need for more instances of similar data collection over time, based on a comparable sampling frame and content of enquiry, if trends are to be examined. Quantitative data need to be based on sufficiently large samples that are, if necessary, weighted in order to include enough members of different groups for comparisons to be valid. In most cases, samples should include both minority and other groups to ensure that conclusions drawn on differences between groups do indeed emerge under comparable conditions. Studies of black and minority ethnic groups alone can be valuable in highlighting circumstances and experiences, but they are not appropriate tools for drawing conclusions about differential advantage and disadvantage.

The interpretation and presentation of findings are indeed particularly crucial, and this applies especially to small studies of young people in particular circumstances. It is important to highlight the plight of any group in need, but it is also essential that it is not concluded that their predicament is unusual, or indeed necessarily typical, without comparative data. An example could be Shah and Hatton's (1999) study of young carers from South Asian communities. This research illustrated the difficulties of accessing services faced by 19 young carers, aged from 8 to 20 years, from 13 households, who were all also in full-time education, and demonstrated how they felt stigmatised and isolated. This study provided a valid illustration of a group in need, but its findings do not have implications for the exclusivity of such need.

It is also very important to distinguish between the *numbers* of young people one might be talking about, and their *representation* within their population group. Children excluded from school are a good example. Although black Caribbean children are almost four times as likely to be excluded as pupils from white backgrounds, they comprise only 5.5 per cent of the total excluded population as compared with the 84.5 per cent accounted for by their white peers.

The Runnymede Trust (Parekh, 2000) is among those to have called for more research on the circumstances and experiences of people from different ethnic backgrounds in Britain. There are many areas in which this could be undertaken in relation to children and young people and include:

- the circumstances and needs of the growing number of young people from mixed-heritage backgrounds;
- the circumstances and needs of young refugees and asylum seekers and the role and effectiveness of services set up to support them;
- the meaning and consequences, as seen by young people themselves, of membership of black and minority ethnic groups in contemporary Britain (in both inner-city environments where their concentrations are high and rural and other settings where their numbers may be small);
- physical health inequalities among young people (including those with disabilities) from diverse backgrounds;
- patterns of mental health (including deliberate self-harm) among young people from black and minority ethnic backgrounds and any identified needs for services;
- educational inequalities and the interaction between ethnicity, poverty, deprived neighbourhoods and educational provision;
- child abuse and child protection issues in relation to children from black and minority ethnic backgrounds;
- experiences of the transition from school to continuing education, training, employment or unemployment according to ethnicity, the factors influencing patterns, the views and expectations of young people about these, and any consequent implications for services or service development;

- the promotion of good relationships among children and young people from diverse backgrounds;
- the differential take-up and use of services (in all areas of interest and concern) by ethnicity, and the reasons for these.

The list could go on.

Developing policy and practice

Determining optimal policy and practice that acknowledges diversity and diverse needs is a massive and complex task. Although it is beyond the scope of this report to provide a comprehensive account of how need might best be met, it is worth reiterating a few critical concerns that have important implications for the welfare and well-being of children and young people.

One crucial question is whether or not the needs of black and minority ethnic young people and their families, and the best ways of meeting these, are the same as for everyone else in the community. Do children from certain backgrounds require 'special' services? Should similar services be provided in a different way? Does take-up need to be facilitated and encouraged? These can be tricky questions for service providers who must not be seen as discriminating unnecessarily and acting in a racially biased manner on the one hand, nor appearing 'colour blind' on the other.

The need for some special services for minority ethnic groups is not disputed. Language tuition for young people not fluent in English, or health care for sickle cell disease or thalassaemia, or a 'culturally appropriate' programme to provide sex education and information on HIV and AIDS (Nelson, 1996), are particularly obvious examples. Moreover, particular groups might want specific types of provision, or might just feel happier sharing an activity with others from a similar cultural background. On the other hand, it is generally argued that the majority of services for minority groups should be part of the mainstream provision, even if additional safeguards against institutional racism, and thinking that the same services will automatically mean equality of outcome, are necessary.

Getting the balance right is paramount. Taking account of race, ethnicity and culture has been highlighted among the most important of the common principles and ways of working which should underpin the practice of all agencies and professionals working to safeguard children and promote their welfare (Department of Health, 1999e). This government report noted:

> it is important that professionals are sensitive to differing family patterns and lifestyles and to child rearing patterns that vary across different racial, ethnic and cultural groups. Professionals should also be aware of the broader social factors that serve to discriminate against black and minority ethnic people ... [be] committed to equality .... understand the effects of racial harassment, racial discrimination and institutional racism, as well as cultural misunderstanding or misinterpretation .... guard against myths and stereotypes ... [and] anxiety about being accused of racist practice should not prevent the necessary action being taken to safeguard a child.

Besides these considerations and recommendations, however, it is important that principles are translated into reality. Most central and local government guidelines on policy and practice now refer to black and minority ethnic groups and the specific provision that should be made for them, but the existence of such guidelines is not sufficient to mean that they are adopted. One problem, it would seem, is the lack of specificity of guidance that must then be interpreted by a service that may never before have had priorities in the area. The Department of Health (2000a), for example, has recently issued practice guidance on assessing children in need and their families which addresses the following two key questions:

> What are the developmental needs of black children and their families, and in what ways are these similar, and in what ways do they differ from the developmental needs of white children and families?

> How can these developmental needs be responded to in work with black children and families?

Although these are discussed, and illustrations provided, it could be argued that provision in practice depends very much on the interpretations and responses of individual service providers. This can suggest that a little more prescription may be what is most needed. Monitoring by ethnicity is another good example. The lack of guidance on the value of monitoring data and how they should be used is frequently given as an important reason why such records are not collected.

Guidelines will have the most impact where they are clear, realistic, feasible and with enough detail to be translated into practice. Ensuring that guidelines for policy and practice are clear is prerequisite to establishing whether they are followed, and whether they are effective in meeting their aims and objectives. More research on issues concerning young people from diverse backgrounds, in combination with greater monitoring by ethnicity, should assist in determining their effectiveness, both in how services are provided and in whether they reach those for whom they are intended.

Monitoring by ethnicity

Monitoring by ethnicity is generally acknowledged as a critical component in any system of comprehensive service delivery for minority ethnic groups which can assist in identifying need, in tracking service provision and take-up, and in evaluating service outcome. Ethnic monitoring can also help to ensure the effective implementation of the requirements of the Race Relations Act (and other legislation and guidance) and:

> guided by a racial equality policy and action plan, will provide crucial information about the workforce and service users, increasing the ability of the service to respond to young people's needs. (CRE, 1995)

Nonetheless, and despite widespread and current recognition of its importance, the need for fuller, more consistent monitoring by ethnicity has been a repeated plea made in relation to: the numbers of young people looked after by local authorities (Utting, 1997), pupil performance at school (Ofsted, 1999), health inequalities among children and young people (Department of Health, 2000h), and the delivery of family support services (Department of Health, 1999a). Factors that seem to have been responsible for the lack of consistency in monitoring are the absence of guidance in this area, the lack of effective mechanisms to put it in place, and the widespread uncertainty about the purpose of monitoring and the ways in which the resultant data can be used.

Significant improvements in monitoring are, however, currently taking place. As outlined above, a range of services including health, education and social services are strengthening practice in this area and becoming better able to report on the characteristics of the young people they support as well as the impact their services appear to be having.

There are, nonetheless, limitations to the quality of monitoring by ethnicity that is generally carried out. First of all, there is no single acceptable way of classifying diverse populations. Ethnicity is a complex and multifaceted concept that can change and develop over time, and which embraces nationality, racial origin, parentage, culture, language and religion on the one hand, and self-perceptions and beliefs on the other. Monitoring, however, is usually done on the basis of Census definitions which fail to take into account factors other than skin colour and country of origin. It could be essential to know about children's language skills, for example, in interpreting their patterns of attainment, and it could be essential to know about religious backgrounds of young people in ascertaining appropriate forms of health service provision.

There remains scope for investigation of how such aspects of language, culture and religion can most usefully be taken into account. An additional need is to examine how the rapidly rising numbers of young people of mixed heritage can best be recorded. There is a strong case for involving young people in these activities to help to ensure that the conclusions drawn are meaningful.

The call for more and better monitoring by ethnicity must, however, be set against the arguments that decry its value. It has been suggested that presentation of information collected in this way can be misleading if taken out of context and may even accentuate hostility through highlighting a particular area, either unintentionally or for political purposes. It may be used to suggest that certain issues (e.g. crime and delinquency) are race-related when in fact they may be more common among white people. Skellington (1996) has also pointed out how it can be argued that few improvements have resulted from the monitoring that has taken place, and that it is possible that sometimes disadvantages have outweighed advantages.

Monitoring is certainly most likely to be useful where it has a specific purpose. The recent development of a range of performance indicators to record specified aspects of circumstances or services in a comparable manner over time (Home Office, 2000b; 2001a) is an important move in this direction. In order 'to provide a clear public statement of what this Government has achieved in promoting race equality, and just as importantly to identify where more needs to be done', information will be monitored in the following areas:

- What people think and feel about three key issues: racial prejudice; service delivery within the public sector; and the public sector as an employer.
- Indicators of service delivery in key policy areas of: economic activity; education; health; law and order; housing; local government; the use of lottery funding; and the voluntary sector.
- The government and its own performance, in modernising the public sector in terms of how policies are devised, how services are delivered to the public, and how all the other functions of government are provided.

The second area listed above draws together existing statistics or develops new measures for children and young people in relation to: employment rates by sex, age and ethnic group of males and females aged 16 to 24 years; the proportion of children living in families below various income thresholds, analysed according to the ethnic group of the head of the household; the proportion of pupils gaining five or more GCSEs at A*- C; rates of permanent exclusions of pupils of compulsory school age as recorded by the Department for Education and Employment Annual School Census; the proportions of 16- to 18-year-olds in and not in education or training by ethnicity as shown by the Youth Cohort Study; the percentage of young people leaving care aged 16 or over with at least one GCSE at grades A* to G or GNVQ; a measure of psychological health (although this will not necessarily apply to young people); and the ethnicity of children in need based on the proportion from different backgrounds living in deprived areas and poor housing.

The Audit Commission has also now included Performance Indicators on ethnicity and racial harassment in their Best Value indicators for local authority service reviews. These include: staff from minority ethnic communities as a percentage of the total workforce; the number of racial incidents recorded by the authority per 100,000 population in any of its services including schools; and the percentage of racial incidents that resulted in further action. New indicators on racial harassment (and refuge provision for victims of domestic violence) will be introduced and include the number of racial incidents recorded by the authority per 100,000 population. It is interesting to note that:

> Racial incidents are any incidents regarded as such by the victim or anyone else. The indicator applies to all an authority's services including schools and to employment by the authority.

In summary, the collection of meaningful information on young people from diverse backgrounds is dependent on good-quality information, and comparisons between groups are, among other things, reliant on the ways in which groups are classified and categorised, the uniformity with which this is done, and the use to which the resultant data are put.

Promoting harmony

It is, however, not enough to carry out high-quality research, promote and evaluate policy and practice in specific areas, and carry out widespread monitoring by ethnicity, if there is not at the same time an overarching commitment and strategy to combat racism and promote harmony within society as a whole. There is clearly no blueprint for this, but the earlier discussion provides pointers towards some of the elements such a strategy might include. These are the need to learn from experience, to address all aspects of young lives, to develop strategies that take account of prejudice and discrimination, and to involve all sections of the community in any actions that are taken.

First, it is important to learn from collective experience and draw on the enormous amount of good practice that has been developed and demonstrated in a wide range of areas affecting children and young people from diverse backgrounds. This report has outlined many recommendations for multicultural education, dealing with racist bullying and crime, recording cultural diversity, and improving services that are neither discriminatory nor colour-blind but take account of individual needs and values. It has stressed the need for clear objectives and standards as well as for appropriate monitoring and the continual re-evaluation of practice and provision.

These strategies have the aim of increasing equity and equality of opportunity and, in principle at least, address the gestalt of young people's lives. The importance of involving families and the local community in activities for young people, 'joined up working' between services, valuing diversity, reducing poverty and social disadvantage, and promoting the self-esteem and positive self-images of all young people whatever their background and circumstances, are frequently iterated objectives.

Nonetheless, there is often the need for an added ingredient to deal with the attitudes and incidents that can block progress in many of these areas. Prejudice and discrimination exist in society, and affect many lives in both measurable and immeasurable ways. There is a lack of effective strategies to combat racism, and such behaviour can arise in the face of what seems to be appropriate policy and practice. Although things have moved on over the past decade, a case in point is made by Macdonald and others (1989) in response to the murder of a pupil at a Manchester school. These authors pointed out how the events at the school could have happened almost anywhere and that the school 'presents a paradox'. It was very committed to anti-racist policies but yet the scene of:

> greater racial conflict and polarisation of its students along racial lines than any other school we have heard of.

It remains a priority to strive to develop more effective ways of reducing intercultural conflict. The assumption is that improving young people's lives generally, and encouraging positive self-images among all young people, will help, but clearly more needs to be done. Sometimes the strategy will be universal, and sometimes it will mean targeting particular groups of perpetrators (Sibbitt, 1997) or localities. According to the authors of the report on Sagaland (Centre for Multicultural Education, 1992), which examined the beliefs and practices of 10- to 14-year-olds in Thamesmead following a number of serious racial incidents:

> Anti-racist work among the younger generation ... must start from the recognition that many of these young people are agitated, confused and disturbed by the history of events surrounding and subsequent to Rolan Adams' murder .... The children in this age group ... believe that everyone who does not live in

> Thamesmead regards them without exception as racists. They are, as they see it, labelled and their futures possibly blighted. Prime architects of this 'world's view' of Thamesmead are the media, especially the press, they say.

Bhavnani (2001) observed how much antiracist work has focused on minority ethnic groups, and how working with black and white groups together is much more rare. It would seem apparent that a reversal of this focus must be an essential element of any future strategies to promote harmony and mutuality within the community.

Conveying the right messages

The need to get the messages right and get them across, is the penultimate conclusion of this report. Among other things, this means ensuring that appropriate information is conveyed to service providers, encouraging responsibility among politicians and the media, giving children and young people a balanced and realistic picture of Britain as a multicultural society, and making sure the messages are correct.

It has been consistently shown how services can lack strategies for working with minority ethnic groups, and for translating principles into practice, despite policies in these areas. It would seem that a failure to understand the purpose of such policies, as well as a lack of commitment to them, is often contributory. O'Neale (2000) reported how many authorities had anti-racist policies and strategies that did not appear to be implemented, and that even where they spoke of 'mainstreaming' the issues it was frequently apparent that nobody took responsibility and they were in effect ignored. Monitoring by ethnicity is often accorded low priority for similar reasons. Reports discussed throughout this review have shown how many schools, authorities and others promote monitoring on the one hand, but yet do not appreciate its purpose nor carry it out on the other.

Similar conclusions apply in other service areas. An examination of eight local authorities providing family support services found that although six of these included equal-opportunity principles in policies and procedures for Children's Services Plans, in only one of these were they:

> championed and promoted by senior managers. The importance of doing so did not appear to be either understood or even accepted by most managers.
> (Department of Health, 1999a)

Often it seems that service providers are influenced by stereotypes of minority groups and offer, or fail to offer, services accordingly (Beresford, 1995; Shah, 1995).

Furthermore, opportunities for taking an initiative are frequently missed. Sibbitt (1997) provided an example from his research study on the perpetrators of racial harassment and racial violence. As he pointed out, most agencies in the study areas had policies on racial harassment and equal opportunities but few had tried to identify or work with potential perpetrators. Information on perpetrators was not collected systematically, and what was collected was rarely collated or shared between agencies. Generally speaking, equal-opportunity and antiracist policies might have a better chance of being implemented if service providers had a better understanding of the rationale behind them as well as the impact they might have.

Part of this message received by service providers is of course that conveyed to society as a whole. Alibhai-Brown (1999) recently discussed the inflammatory impact of media reports and politicians' comments and put forward the view that the government needs to take direct action on the attitudes that lie behind discriminatory behaviour. Her views are supported by research (Audit Commission, 2000b; Fekete, 2001) outlining how coverage of refugees and asylum seekers has, in particular, been highly negative. Alibhai-Brown wrote:

> The damaging effects of contradictory messages about immigrants and about black and Asian Britons have rarely been considered. Mixed messages have been given out by politicians and the tendency has been to follow public prejudice rather than lead, change and inform public opinion. Insufficient attention has been given to the need for coherent integration policies which would influence public attitudes and educate the population – black and white – on the realities of multicultural Britain and the changes that have taken place in the demographics, cultural and political life of their country. Myths have settled and rarely been challenged until politicians began, in recent years, to inject some balance into the debate by drawing attention to the positive contribution which immigrants, refugees and members of minority communities have made.

> White Britons are not a homogenous group. The diversity of opinion, emerging identities, attitudes to racial minorities and multiculturalism within the majority community needs to be studied. Research into this 'new' area should be instigated by the Government. There is a need to find out, for instance, what influences attitudes towards multiculturalism if a strategy to influence those attitudes is to be successful.

Her thesis is that the government should take a definite lead in trying to provide realistic and positive messages about the contribution of minority ethnic groups, and the importance of respect and acceptance. The strategy should be one of public education which, through the media, seeks to promote intercultural understanding.

Something along these lines is currently being planned in relation to young people. As outlined by the Home Secretary (Home Office, 2001b), the National Curriculum is being amended to include Citizenship, aimed at valuing cultural diversity and preventing racism. This is being introduced as a statutory subject in secondary schools from September 2002 and as a non-statutory subject in primary schools two years earlier. For the first time, all pupils will be taught about the diversity of national, regional, religious and ethnic identities in Britain and the need for mutual respect and understanding. They will also be instructed about prejudice and stereotypes, as well as on how to challenge racism and bullying. A Citizenship website, available from summer 2001, will include related materials for pupils, parents and teachers. These moves were supported by both the Stephen Lawrence Inquiry (Macpherson, 1999) and the recent Bradford Race Review (Ouseley, 2001). Their implementation and impact, however, remain to be seen.

Providing the right messages for young people needs to start as early as possible (Lane, 1999) and be conveyed through the pre-school years, at school, via the community, in the media, and in every other possible context. All messages in all contexts should be consistent both with each other and with images of society. The celebration of mixed heritage, for example, might sit unhappily against a paucity of role models of white mothers with black children in the media (Katz, 1996), just as the advocacy of equal opportunities can be seen to be at some variance with the demonstrated inequality of high-status occupations according to ethnicity (Home Office, 2000b). Messages about the meaning of ethnicity should also not focus on disadvantage and discrimination to the exclusion of achievement and harmony, but should attain a realistic balance which reflects society and its members with both problems and triumphs.

Listening to young people

Finally, it is important to stress the value and equity of taking young views into account. Listening to young people in the process of service development, and finding out what they think, are key issues; young people's own personal priorities, involving representative groups of young people in reaching solutions to local difficulties, and getting their feedback as things change, are all crucial. Consultation can take many forms, from published personal stories (Kassam, 1997) to surveys of young people (Bentley and others, 1999) to initiatives such as the Black Youth Charter (National Black Youth Forum, 1999). This forum, a group of black young people aged from 13 to 25 years from African and Asian backgrounds, consulted 200 youth organisations in a range of areas (education; employment; health; the media; family and communities;

culture; environment; facilities; police, the law and the judiciary; immigration and asylum issues; and politics) and produced a list of 80 rights and recommendations which included:

> We want a cross-department Minister for Black Young People to promote our issues and concerns and ensure equality across legislation.

Children's Express, which promotes learning through journalism for children aged between 8 and 18 years, is another good example. This has produced a number of articles addressing black and minority issues from the personal perspectives of young people. One article (*Children's Express,* 1999), for example, described 'the black experience' through asking young people to talk about their encounters with racism on the streets of London. This is not a mechanism for collecting the views of a representative group of young people, but it is an important avenue for giving young people a say and letting their views be known more widely.

There is, however, also a need to understand from young people more generally just what ethnicity means for young lives. At present there is no representative perspective on many questions and issues. What do young people think about their own and others' identity and ethnicity, what do they know about ethnicity and diversity in Britain, do they feel that certain groups in society are more advantaged or disadvantaged than others, and in what ways would they say their own background affects and has affected their own lives? Information on these themes from a large-scale survey of young people from a wide range of backgrounds would provide useful pointers for policy and practice development.

The commitment to consulting children and young people has gained enormous currency in recent years. Children's participation is enshrined in many initiatives led by both government bodies and voluntary organisations, and young views are recognised as having real significance in the development of policy and practice. All young people, whatever their background, ethnicity or culture, should have opportunities to participate in decisions affecting them, and it is partly through these that the way forward lies. Opportunities, nonetheless, do not necessarily translate into reality. It is important to encourage young people to respond honestly and constructively to the chance to say what they think and to ensure that those in a position to 'do something' take their views and perspectives fully into account.

> Adults never understand anything for themselves, and it is tiresome for children to be always and forever explaining things to them

complained Le Petit Prince. That may be true, but let's hope that they continue to have patience.

References

Abebaw, M, Abdi, F, Ahamad, D, Goitom, M, Rehane, A, Tesfaye, D and Yohannes, B (1998) *Let's Spell It Out. Hays Horn of Africa Youth Scheme*. In partnership with Save the Children Fund

Acheson, D (1998) *Independent Inquiry into Inequalities in Mental Health*. HMSO

Ahmad, W and Atkin, K (1996) Ethnicity and Caring for a Disabled Child: The case of children with sickle cell or thalassaemia, *British Journal of Social Work*, 26, 755–75

Alexander, Z (1999) *Study of Black, Asian and Ethnic Minority Issues*. DoH

Alexander, Z and Dewjee, A (1981) *Roots in Britain. Black and Asian citizens from Elizabeth I to Elizabeth II*. Brent Library Service

Alibhai-Brown, Y (1999) *True Colours. Public Attitudes to Multiculturalism and the Role of the Government*. Institute for Public Policy Research

Alibhai-Brown, Y (2001) *Mixed Feelings: The complex lives of mixed-race Britons*. Women's Press

Amin, K, Drew, D, Fosam, B, Gillborn, D and Demack, S (1997) *Black and Ethnic Minority Young People and Educational Disadvantage*. Runnymede Trust

Anionwu, E (1996) Sickle cell and Thalassaemia: some priorities for nursing, *Journal of Advanced Nursing*, 23, 5, 853–6

Anwar, M (1998) *Between Cultures: Continuity and change in the lives of young Asians*. Routledge

Aspinall, P (2000) The Challenges of Measuring the Ethno-cultural Diversity of Britain in the New Millennium, *Policy & Politics*, 28, 1, 109–18

Association of London Government (1998) 'Unpublished data on refugees and asylum seekers being assisted by London Boroughs' *in* Hargreaves, S, Bardsley, M, Barker, M, Kenny, D, Morgan, D, Roberts, I and Streetly, A (1999) *Child Health in London. The health and social characteristics of London's children*. The Health of Londoners Project

Association of Metropolitan Authorities (1994) *Special Child – Special Needs: Services for children with disabilities*. LMB Publications

Atkin, K and Rollings, J (1993) *Community Care in a Multi-Racial Britain*. HMSO

Audit Commission (1999) *Making Connections: Learning the lessons from Joint Reviews, 1998/9*. Department of Health, Social Services Inspectorate, and National Assembly for Wales. Audit Commission

Audit Commission (2000a) *A New City: Supporting asylum seekers and refugees in London*. Audit Commission

Audit Commission (2000b) *Another Country: Implementing dispersal under the Immigration and Asylum Act 1999*. Audit Commission

Bagley, C (1971) Mental Illness in Immigrant Minorities in London, *Journal of Biosocial Sciences,* 3, 449–60

Bagley, C and Young, L 'The identity, adjustment and achievement of "transracially" adopted children: a review and empirical report' *in* Verma, C and Bagley, G *eds* (1979) *Race, Education and Identity.* Macmillan

Baker, P and Eversley, J *eds* (2000) *Multilingual Capital: The languages of London's school children and their relevance to economic, social and educational policies.* Battlebridge Publications

Banton, M (1987) *Racial Theories.* Cambridge University Press

Barclay, G and Mhlanga, B (2000) *Ethnic Differences in Decisions on Young Defendants dealt with by the Crown Prosecution Service.* Home Office Section 95 Findings No. 1

Bardsley, M, Hamm, J, Lowdell, C, Morgan, D and Storkey, M (2000) *Developing Health Assessment for Black and Ethnic Minority Groups.* NHS Executive

Barn, R, Sinclair, R and Ferdinand, D (1997) *Acting On Principle: An examination of race and ethnicity in social services provision for children and families.* BAAF

Barnardo's (2000) *Children First and Foremost: Meeting the needs of unaccompanied, asylum-seeking children.* Barnardo's

Barter, C (1999) *Protecting Children from Racism and Racial Abuse: A research review.* NSPCC

Bastiani, J (2000) *Supplementary Schooling in the Lambeth Education Action Zone.* CfBT/Lambeth EAZ

Baxter, C (1989) Parent-perceived attitudes of professionals: implications for service providers, *Disability, Handicap & Society,* 4, 259–69

Bebbington, A and Miles, J (1989) The background of children who enter local authority care, *British Journal of Social Work,* 19, 5, 349–68

Beishon, S, Modood, T and Virdee, S (1998) *Ethnic Minority Families.* Policy Studies Institute

Benjamin, F (undated) *Heart of Learning. Supporting children in the Foundation Stage.* 75 minutes video. EYTARN

Bennetto, J (2000) Drug addiction is surging among Asian community, *The Independent,* 10 January

Bentley, T and Oakley, K with Gibson, S and Kilgour, K (1999) *The Real Deal: What young people really think about government, politics and social exclusion.* Demos

Beresford, B (1995) *Expert Opinions: Families with severely disabled children.* Joseph Rowntree Foundation

Berthoud, R (1999) *Young Caribbean Men and the Labour Market: A comparison with other ethnic groups.* Joseph Rowntree Foundation

Berthoud, R (2000) *Family Formation in Multi-Cultural Britain: Three patterns of diversity.* Working Paper 2000–34, Institute for Social & Economic Research, University of Essex

Berthoud, R (2001) Teenage births to ethnic minority women, *Population Trends* 104, 12–17. National Statistics

Bhatti, G (1999) *Asian Children at Home and at School: An ethnographic study.* Routledge

Bhavnani, R (2001) *Rethinking Interventions In Racism.* Commission for Racial Equality/Trentham Books

Bhugra, D (undated) 'Deliberate self harm in ethnic minority adolescents' Abstract on NHS executive website

Bignall, T and Butt, J (2000) *Between Ambition and Achievement: Young black disabled people's views and experiences of independence and independent living.* Policy Press

Black Peoples Progressive Association and Redbridge Community Relations Council (1978) *Cause For Concern: West Indian pupils in Redbridge.* BPPA & RCRC

Black Regeneration Forum (2000) *Minority Ethnic Issues in Social Exclusion and Neighbourhood Renewal.* Black Regeneration Forum

Blair, M and Bourne, J (1998) *Making the Difference: Teaching and learning strategies in successful multi-ethnic schools.* DfEE

Bose, R 'Families in transition' *in* Lau, A *ed.* (2000) *South Asian Children and Adolescents in Britain.* Whurr Publishers

Bridge Child Care Consultancy Services (1991) *Sukina: An evaluation report of events leading up to her death.* The Bridge

British Broadcasting Corporation (2000) *Guidelines for Producers.* BBC

Broadcasting Standards Commission (1998) *Codes of Guidance.* BSC

Buckingham, D, Davies, H, Jones, K and Kelley, P (1999) *Children's Television in Britain: History, discourse and policy.* British Film Institute

Busari, S (2000) What can black family day mean if you're young, black and homeless? *New Nation,* 11 September 2000, 6–7

Butt, J and Box, L (1998) *Family Centred: A study of the use of family centres by black families.* Race Equality Unit

Cabinet Office (2000a) *Minority Ethnic Issues in Social Exclusion and Neighbourhood Renewal: A guide to the work of the Social Exclusion Unit and the Policy Action Teams so far.* TSO

Cabinet Office (2000b) *National Strategy for Neighbourhood Renewal: Report of Policy Action Team 12: Young People.* www.cabinet-office.gov.uk/seu/2000/pat12/annex-c.htm

Cabinet Office (2001) *Improving labour market achievements for ethnic minorities in British society.* www.cabinet-office.gov.uk/innovation/2001/ethnicity/scope.shtml

Centre for Housing Policy (1993) *Single Homeless People* University of York

Centre for Multicultural Education (Institute of Education) (1992) *Sagaland: Youth culture, racism and education.* The Central Race Equality Unit of the London Borough of Greenwich and Greenwich Education Service

Centrepoint (2000) *Statistics on homelessness*

Chahal, K and Julienne, L (1999) *'We Can't All Be White!' Racist victimisation in the UK.* Joseph Rowntree Foundation

Chamba, R, Ahmad, W, Hirst, M, Lawton, D and Beresford, B (1999) *On the Edge. Minority ethnic families caring for a severely disabled child.* Policy Press and Joseph Rowntree Foundation

Chand, A (2000) The over representation of Black children in the child protection system, *Child and Family Social Work,* 5, 67–77

Channer, Y and Parton, N (1990) *Taking Child Abuse Seriously.* Unwin Hyman

ChildLine (1996) *Children and Racism.* ChildLine

Children and Young People's Unit (2001) *Children's Fund. Part Two Guidance.* CYPU

Children's Express (1999) The black experience. Young people talk about their encounters with racism on the streets of London, *The Guardian,* 25 February, 22

Clark, K B and Clark, M P 'Racial identification and preference in Negro children' *in* Newcomb, T M and Hartley, E L *eds* (1947) *Readings in Social Psychology.* Henry Holt

Coard, B (1971) *How the West Indian Child is made Educationally Sub-Normal in the British School System.* Caribbean Education and Caribbean Workers' Association and New Beacon Books

Cohen, P and Gardner, C (1982) *It Aint Half Racist Mum: Fighting racism in the media*. Comedia Publishing

Commission for Racial Equality (1985) *First Review of the Race Relations Act 1976*. CRE

Commission for Racial Equality (1991) *Consultation Draft: Race Relations Code of Practice for the elimination of racial discrimination and the promotion of equal opportunity in the provision of mental health services*. CRE

Commission for Racial Equality (1992) *Second Review of the Race Relations Act 1976*. CRE

Commission for Racial Equality (1995) *Young and Equal: A standard for racial equality in services working with young people*. CRE

Commission for Racial Equality (1996) *From Cradle To School*. CRE

Commission for Racial Equality (1998a) *Reform of the Race Relations Act 1976: Proposals for change submitted by the Commission for Racial Equality to the Rt Hon Jack Straw MP, Secretary of State for the Home Department, on 30 April 1998*. CRE

Commission for Racial Equality (1998b) *Stereotyping and Racism*. CRE

Commission for Racial Equality (1999) *Ethnic Minorities in Britain*. CRE Factsheet

Community Health South London (2000) Research into the needs of young refugees in Lambeth, Southwark and Lewisham, *Young People's Health Network*, 13

Community Relations Commission (1976) *Between Two Cultures: A study of the relationships between generations in the Asian community in Britain*. CRC

Connexions (2000) *The Best Start in Life for Every Young Person*. DfEE

Connolly, P (1998) *Racism, Gender Identities and Young Children*. Routledge

Cooper, H, Smaje, C and Arber, S (1998) Use of health services by children and young people according to ethnicity and social class: secondary analysis of a national survey, *British Medical Journal*, 317, 1047–50

Creighton, S (1992) *Child Abuse Trends in England and Wales 1988–1990. An overview from 1973– 1990*. NSPCC

Daycare Trust (2000) *Ensuring Equality*. Daycare Trust

Demaine, J ed. (2001) *Sociology of Education Today*. Palgrave

Department for Education and Employment (1997) *Survey of Parents of Three and Four Year Old Children and Their Use of Early Years Services*. DfEE

Department for Education and Employment (1998) *Meeting the Childcare Challenge*. HMSO

Department for Education and Employment (1999a) *Social Inclusion: Pupil Support. The Secretary of State's guidance on pupil attendance, behaviour, exclusion and re-integration. Circulars 10/99 and 11/99*. DfEE

Department for Education and Employment (1999b) *Statistics of Education. Schools in England*. DfEE

Department for Education and Employment (2000a) *Consultation on Guidance for Schools on Ethnic Monitoring*. DfEE

Department for Education and Employment (2000b) *Implementation of the Teenage Pregnancy Strategy*. Progress report, November. DfEE

Department for Education and Employment (2000c) *Permanent Exclusions and Exclusion Appeals, England 1998/9* (provisional)

Department for Education and Employment (2000d) *Removing the Barriers: Raising achievement levels for minority ethnic pupils*. DfEE

Department for Education and Employment (2000e) *Schools Plus: Building Learning Communities – Improving the Educational Chances of Children and Young People from Disadvantaged Areas*. DfEE

Department for Education and Employment (2000f) *Statistics of Education: Pupil absence and truancy from schools in England, 1999/2000*. DfEE

Department for Education and Employment (2000g) *Statistics of Education: Schools in England 2000*. The Stationery Office

Department for Education and Employment (2001a) *Early Years Development and Childcare Partnership Planning Guidance 2001–2002*. DfEE

Department for Education and Employment (2001b) *Promoting Play in Out-of-school Childcare. Good Practice for EYDC Partnerships*. DfEE

Department for Education and Employment (2001c) *Youth Cohort Study: The Activities and Experiences of 18 Year Olds: England and Wales 2000*. SFR 03/2001. DfEE

Department for Education and Employment (2001d) *Youth Cohort Study: The Activities and Experiences of 16 Year Olds: England and Wales 2000*. SFR 02/2001. DfEE

Department of the Environment, Transport and the Regions (1998) *1998 Index of Local Deprivation. A summary of results*. DETR

Department of Health (1996) *Directory of Ethnic Minority Initiatives*. DoH

Department of Health (1998a) *Adoption – achieving the right balance*. LAC(98)20

Department of Health (1998b) *Directory of African Caribbean Initiatives*. DoH

Department of Health (1998c) *Directory of Asian Initiatives*. DoH

Department of Health (1998d) *Directory of Ethnic Minority Initiatives*. Vol 2, May 1998. DoH

Department of Health (1998e) *Modernising Mental Health services: Safe, sound and supportive*. DoH

Department of Health (1999a) *Getting Family Support Right*. TSO

Department of Health (1999b) *National Service Framework for Mental Health: Modern standard and service models*. DoH

Department of Health (1999c) *Teenage Pregnancy*. DoH

Department of Health (1999d) *The Government's Objectives for Children's Social Services*. TSO

Department of Health (1999e) *Working Together to Safeguard Children: A guide to inter-agency working to safeguard and promote the welfare of children*. TSO

Department of Health (2000a) *Assessing Children in Need and their Families: Practice guidance*. TSO

Department of Health (2000b) *Black and Ethnic Nurses, Midwives and Health Visitors Leading Change*. DoH

Department of Health (2000c) *Promoting Health for Looked After Children: A guide to healthcare planning, assessment and monitoring. Consultation document*. DoH

Department of Health (2000d) *Quality Protects: Analysis of management action plans with reference to disabled children and families*. DoH

Department of Health (2000e) *Social Services Performance in 1999–2000: The Personal Social Services Performance Assessment Framework Indicators*. DoH

Department of Health (2000f) *The Children Act Report*. DoH

Department of Health (2000g) 'The Quality Protects Programme: transforming children's services 2001–2002' *Local Authority Circular, series number LAC (2000) 22*. DoH

Department of Health (2000h) *The Race Equality Agenda of the Department of Health*. DoH

Department of Health (2000i) *Tracking Progress in Children's Services: An evaluation of local responses to the Quality Protects Programme.* DoH

Department of Health (2001a) *Children in Need Census.* DoH

Department of Health (2001b) *Co-ordinated Service Planning for Vulnerable Children and Young People in England.* Social Services Inspectorate

Department of Health (2001c) *Ethnicity. Collection of ethnic data in DH central statistical collections: a 'position statement' update: January 2001.* www.doh.gov.uk./ethdevlist3.htm

Department of Health (2001d) *The Children Act Report 2000.* DoH

Department of Health (2001e) *Valuing People: A new strategy for learning disability for the 21st century: a white paper.* DoH

Disability Rights Task Force (1999) *From Exclusion to Inclusion.* HMSO

Dorkenoo, E (1994) *Cutting the Rose: Female genital mutilation: The practice and its prevention.* Minority Rights Publications

Dorsett, R (1998) *Ethnic Minorities in the Inner City.* Joseph Rowntree Foundation

Dosanjh, J and Ghuman P (1998) Child Rearing Practices of Two Generations of Punjabi Parents: development of personality and independence, *Children and Society*, 12, 25–37

Dummett, A and Martin, I (1982) *British Nationality: The AGIN guide to the new law.* National Council for Civil Liberties

Earley, P and others (1999) *Improving the Effectiveness of School Governing Bodies.* DfEE

Early Years Trainers Anti Racist Network (1996) *On The Spot: Dealing with racism.* EYTARN

Early Years Trainers Anti Racist Network (1999) *Inspecting for Excellence: A guidance on inspecting for equality in early years settings.* EYTARN

Emerson, E and Azmi, A (1997) *Improving Services for Asian People with Learning Disabilities and their Families.* Hester Adrian Research Centre

Erens, B, Primastesta, P and Prior, G (2001) *Health Survey for England: The health of minority ethnic groups 1999.* TSO

Eslea, M and Mukhtar, K (2000) Bullying and racism among Asian schoolchildren in Britain, *Educational Research*, 42, 2, 207–17

European Commission Against Racism and Intolerance (2001) *Second Report on the United Kingdom. Adopted 16 June 2000.* Council of Europe

European Council on Refugees and Exiles (1996) Position on refugee children by the European Council on Refugees and Exiles, *Childright*, 132

Farmer, E and Owen, M (1995) *Child Protection Practice: Private risks and public remedies, a study of decision-making, intervention and outcome in child protection work.* HMSO

Farrington, D P (1996) *Understanding and Preventing Youth Crime. Social policy research 93.* Joseph Rowntree Foundation

Farrington, D P 'Human development and criminal careers' *in* Maguire, M, Morgan, R and Reiner, R eds (1997) *The Oxford Handbook of Criminology.* Clarendon

Fatimilehin, I and Nadirshaw, Z (1994) A cross-cultural study of parental attitudes and beliefs about learning disability, *Mental Handicap Research*, 7, 202–27

Fekete, L (2001) *The Dispersal of Xenophobia.* Institute of Race Relations

File, N and Power, C (1981) *Black Settlers in Britain 1555–1958.* Heinemann Educational

Finkelhor, D (1986) *A Sourcebook on Child Sexual Abuse.* Sage

FitzGerald, M (1993) *Ethnic Minorities and The Criminal Justice System*. Home Office

FitzGerald, M (1999) Metropolitan police are misusing the power to stop and search suspects, *The Times*, 15 December

FitzGerald, M and Sibbitt R (1997) *Ethnic Monitoring in Police Forces: A beginning*. Home Office Research Study 173

Fitzgerald, R, Finch, S and Nove, A (2000) *Black Caribbean Young Men's Experiences of Education and Employment: Research Brief No 186*. DfEE

Foster, P (1990) *Policy and Practice in Multicultural and Anti-Racist Education*. Routledge

Francome, C (1994) *The Great Leap. Findings on Contemporary Society*. Middlesex University

Franklin, A and Madge, N (2000) *In Our View. Children, teenagers and parents talk about services for young people*. National Children's Bureau

Fryer, P (1984) *Staying Power: The history of black people in Britain*. Pluto Press

Gallagher, B (1998) *Grappling with Smoke: Investigation and managing organised child sexual abuse: A good practice guide*. NSPCC

Ghazala, A, Nocon, A, Ahmad, W and Jones, L (2001) *Learning Difficulties and Ethnicity*. DoH

Ghuman, P (1999) *Asian Adolescents in The West*. British Psychological Society

Gibbons, J, Conroy, S and Bell, C (1995) *Operating Child Protection Policies in English Local Authorities*. HMSO

Giddens, A (1993) *Sociology*. Polity Press

Gill, O and Jackson, B (1983) *Adoption and Race: Black, Asian and Mixed Race Children in White Families*. Batsford Academic and Educational in association with BAAF

Gillborn, D (1990) *'Race' Ethnicity and Education: Teaching and learning in multi-ethnic schools*. Unwin Hyman

Gillborn, D (1995) *Racism and Antiracism in Real Schools: Theory, policy and practice*. Buckingham, Open University Press

Gillborn, D (1996) *Viewpoint, 5: Exclusions from school*. University of London Institute of Education

Gillborn, D and Gipps, C (1996) *Recent Research on the Achievements of Ethnic Minority Pupils*. Ofsted Reviews of Research. HMSO

Gillborn, D and Mirza, H (2000) *Mapping Race, Class and Gender: A synthesis of research evidence*. Ofsted

Gillborn, D and Youdell, D (2000) *Policy, Practice, Reform and Equity*. Open University Press

Goddard, N, Subotsky, F and Fombonne, E (1996) Ethnicity and adolescent deliberate self-harm, *Journal of Adolescence*, 19, 513–21

Goodman, M E (1952) *Race Awareness in Young Children*. Addison-Wesley

Goodman, R and Richards, H (1995) Child and adolescent psychiatric presentations of second generation Afro-Caribbeans in Britain, *British Journal of Psychiatry*, 167, 362–9

Gordon, P 'Racist harassment and violence' *in* Stanko, E A *ed*. (1994) *Perspectives on Violence*. Howard League

Goulbourne, H (1998) *Race Relations in Britain Since 1945*. Macmillan

Graham, J and Bowling, B (1995) *Young People and Crime*. Home Office Research Study 145

Hackett, L, Hackett, P and Taylor, D (1991) Psychological disturbance and its associations in the children of Gujarati community, *Journal of Child Psychology and Psychiatry*, 32, 851–6

Hansard (2000) Child Asylum Seekers, *House of Commons* 360, 10, 138–40

Harland, J and Kinder, K (1999) *Crossing the Line: Extending young people's access to cultural venues.* Gulbenkian Foundation

Harland, J, Kinder, K and Hartley, K (1995) *Arts in Their View: A study of youth participation in the arts.* National Foundation for Educational Research

Harris, P (2001) Far right picks the next race target, *Observer*, 1 July, 10

Haslam, J (2001) Harsh troth, *Guardian Society*, 14 March, 6–7

Health Education Authority (1997) *Young People and Physical Activity: Promoting better practice.* Health Education Authority

Health of Londoners Project (1999) *Refugee Health in London.* Health of Londoners Project

Henderson, P, and Kaur, R (1999) *Rural Racism in the UK.* Community Development Foundation

Hengst, H (1997) Negotiating 'us' and 'them': Children's constructions of collective identity, *Childhood*, 4 ,1, 43–62

Herbert, I (2000) British Asians are warned over risks to children of intermarriage, *Independent*, 5 May

Hodes, M (1998) Refugee children may need a lot of psychiatric help, *British Medical Journal* 316, 793–4

Hodes, M, Creamer, J and Woolley, J (1998) The cultural meanings of ethnic categories, *Psychiatric Bulletin*, 22, 20–4

Home Office (1997) *Racial Violence and Harassment: A Consultation Document.* Home Office

Home Office (1998) *Entry Into the Criminal Justice System: A survey of police arrests and their outcomes.* Home Office Research Study 185

Home Office (1999) *Statistics of Race and the Criminal Justice System.* Home Office

Home Office (2000a) *A Choice by Right: Summary of the report of the working group on forced marriage.* Home Office

Home Office (2000b) *Race Equality in Public Services.* Home Office

Home Office (2001a) *Race Equality in Public Services.* Home Office

Home Office (2001b) *Stephen Lawrence Inquiry. Home Secretary's Action Plan, Second Annual Report on Progress.* Home Office

Independent Television Commission (2001) *Boxed In*

Inner London Education Authority (1969) *Literacy Survey: Summary of interim results of the study of pupils reading standards.* ILEA document

Inner London Education Authority (1973) *Literacy Survey: 1971 follow-up, preliminary report.* ILEA document

Inner London Education Authority (1983a) *Race, Sex and Class 1. Achievement in Schools.* ILEA

Inner London Education Authority (1983b) *Race, Sex and Class 2. Multi-Ethnic Education in Schools.* ILEA

Institute of Race Relations (2001a) *Counting The Cost: Racial violence since Macpherson.* A report from the Institute of Race Relations to London Boroughs Grants

Institute of Race Relations (2001b) Racially motivated murders (known or suspected) since 1991. Online resources at www.homebeats.co.uk/resources/deaths.htm

Irvine, Lord (1999) Guide on the Judicial Studies Board, *The Telegraph*, 1 October

Ivaldi, G (2000) *Surveying Adoption: A comprehensive analysis of local authority adoptions 1998–1999.* British Agencies for Adoption and Fostering

Jacobson, B (2001) *The London Health Strategy Recommendations.* Paper presented at Capita conference

Jadhav, S (1996) The cultural origins of western depression, *International Journal of Social Psychiatry*, 42, 4, 269–86

Joly, D with Kelly, K and Nettleton, C (1997) *Refugees in Europe: The hostile new agenda.* Minority Rights Group International

Jones, E and McCurdy K (1992) The links between child maltreatment and demographic characteristics of children, *Child Abuse and Neglect*, 16

Jowell, R, Brook, L, Taylor, B and Prior, G eds (1995) *British Social Attitudes: the 12th Report.* Dartmouth Publishing

Kassam, N ed. (1997) *Telling It Like It Is: Young Asian women talk.* The Women's Press

Katz, I (1996) *The Construction of Racial Identity in Children of Mixed Parentage.* Jessica Kingsley

Khan, J (2001) Quality Protects, *Special Children* no. 137, 29–30

Kinder, K, Halsey, K and Kendall, S (2000) *Working Out Well: Effective provision for excluded pupils.* NFER

Kohli, R (2000) Issues for social work with unaccompanied asylum seeking children, *Children's Residential Care Unit Newsletter*, 14, 8–10

Kopraska, J and Stein, M 'The Mental Health of Looked After Young People' in Aggleton, P, Hurry, J, Warwick I eds (2000) *Young People and Mental Health.* John Wiley

Kramer, T, Evans, N and Garralda, M E (2000) Ethnic diversity among children and adolescent psychiatric (CAP) clinic attenders, *Child Psychology and Psychiatry Review*, 5, 4, 169–75

Laishley, J (1971) Skin colour awareness and preference in London nursery-school children, *Race*, 13, 47–64

Lane, J (1999) *Action for Racial Equality in the Early Years: Understanding the past, thinking about the present, planning for the future.* National Early Years Network

LASSL (2000) *New Guidance on Children's Services Planning.* LASSL (2000) 3. DoH

Lau, A (2000) *South Asian Children and Adolescents in Britain.* Whurr

La Valle, I, Finch, S, Nove, A and Lewin, C (2000) *Parents' Demand For Childcare Research Brief No 176.* DfEE

Little, A, Mabey C and Whitaker, G (1968) The education of immigrant children in Inner London primary schools, *Race*, 9, 439–52

Little, J and Nicoll, A (1988) The epidemiology and service implications of congenital and constitutional anomalies in ethnic minorities in the United Kingdom, *Paediatric and Perinatal Epidemiology*, 2, 161–84

Littlewood, R (1992) Psychiatric diagnosis and racial bias: empirical and interpretative approaches, *Social Science and Medicine*, 34, 2, 141–9

Lomas, G (1973) *Census 1971: The coloured population of Great Britain: Preliminary report.* Runnymede Trust

London Borough of Lambeth (1987) *Whose Child? The report of the panel appointed to inquire into the death of Tyra Henry.* London Borough of Lambeth

Mac an Ghaill, M (1988) *Young, Gifted and Black: Student-teacher relations in the schooling of black youth.* Open University Press

McCarraher, L (1998) *Family Viewing: A report of the research project into parents, children and the media*. Parenting Education Support Forum

Macdonald, I, Bhavnani, R, Khan, L and John, G (1989) *Murder in The Playground: The Report of the Macdonald Inquiry into racism and racial violence in Manchester schools (The Burnage Report)*. Longsight Press

McDonald, J (1995) *Entitled to Learn? A report on young refugees' experiences of access and progression in the UK education system*. World University Service

MacDonald, S (1991) *All Equal Under the Act: A practical guide to the Children Act 1989 for social workers*. Race Equality Unit

McGibben, L and others (1992) Deliberate self-poisoning in Asian and Caucasian 12–15 year olds, *British Journal of Psychiatry*, 161, 110–2

Macpherson, W (1999) *The Stephen Lawrence Inquiry*. TSO

Madge, N (1976) Context and the expressed ethnic preferences of infant school children, *Journal of Child Psychology and Psychiatry*, 17, 337–44

Madge, N (1997) *Abuse and Survival: A fact file*. The Prince's Trust – Action

Malik, H (1998) *A Practical Guide to Equal Opportunities*. Stanley Thornes

Mason, D (2000) *Race and Ethnicity in Modern Britain*. OUP

Meltzer, H (1994) *Day Care Services for Children*. HMSO

Meltzer, H, Gatward, R, Goodman, R and Ford, T (2000) *Mental Health of Children and Adolescents in Great Britain*. The Stationery Office

Mental Health Foundation (1995) *Mental Health in Black and Minority Ethnic People: The fundamental facts*. Mental Health Foundation

Merrill, J and Owens, J (1986) Ethnic differences in self-poisoning: a comparison of Asian and white groups, *British Journal of Psychiatry*, 148, 708–12

Metropolitan Police (2000) *Policing Diversity: One year on from the publication of the Stephen Lawrence Inquiry Report*. Directorate of Public Affairs

Milner, D (1970) *Ethnic Identity and Preference in Minority-Group Children*. Unpublished Ph.D dissertation, University of Bristol

Milner, D (1983) *Children and Race Ten Years On*. Ward Lock Educational

Modood, T, Berthoud, R and Lakey, J (1997) *Ethnic Minorities in Britain: Diversity and disadvantage*. Policy Studies Institute

Moffatt, P G and Thoburn, J (2001) Outcomes of permanent family placement for children of minority ethnic origin, *Child and Family Social Work*, 6, 13–21

Moghal, N E, Nota, I K and Hobbs, C J (1995) A study of sexual abuse in an Asian community, *Archives of Disease in Childhood*, 72, 4, 346–7

Mullix, M (1998) *Home nursing services for children – an option for minority ethnic children*. Unpublished M.Sc. dissertation

NACRO (1999) *Let's Get It Right: Race and Justice 2000*. NACRO

Nagra, J S (1981/2) *A Teacher's Guide to Multicultural Education*. Basil Blackwell

National Black Youth Forum (1999) *Black Youth Charter*. National Black Youth Forum

National Commission of Inquiry into the Prevention of Child Abuse (1996) *Childhood Matters: Report of the National Commission of Inquiry into the Prevention of Child Abuse, Volume 1 and Volume 2*. Stationery Office

National Union of Schoolmasters/Union of Women Teachers (1999) *Education and Race*. NASUWT

Neeleman, J, Wilson-Jones, C, and Wessely, S (2001) Ethnic density and deliberate self harm; A small area study in south east London, *Journal of Epidemiology and Community Health*, 55, 85–90

Nelson, F (1996) It's a family affair, *Healthlines*, 36, 22–3

Newham Refugee Centre (1997) *Who is That Pupil? A study of services for refugee students in Newham's primary and secondary schools*. Newham Refugee Centre

NHS Executive (1999) *Addressing Black and Minority Ethnic Health in London – A review and recommendations*. London Regional Office of the NHS Executive

Norton, R and Cohen, B (2000) *Out of Exile: Developing youth work with young refugees*. National Youth Agency

Office for National Statistics (1996) *Social Focus on Ethnic Minorities*. HMSO

Office for National Statistics (1997) *Mortality Statistics: Perinatal and infant: social and biological factors, Series DH3*. TSO

Office for National Statistics (2000) *National Population Projections: Report giving population projections by sex and age for the United Kingdom, Great Britain and constituent countries*. TSO

Ofsted (1999) *Raising the Attainment of Minority Ethnic Pupils – School and LEA responses*. Ofsted

Ofsted (2001) *Improving Attendance and Behaviour in Secondary schools*. Ofsted

Okitikpi, T 'Educational needs of black children in the care system' *in* Barn, R *ed*. (1999) *Working with Black Children and Adolescents in Need*. British Agencies for Adoption and Fostering

Okitikpi, T and Aymer, C (2000) Caring for looked after refugee children, *Children's Residential Care Unit Newsletter*, 14 (Autumn), 6–8

O'Neale, V (2000) *Excellence Not Excuses: Inspection of services for ethnic minority children and families*. DoH

Osler, A and Morrison, M (2000) *Inspecting Schools For Race Equality: OFSTED's Strengths and Weaknesses. A report for the Commission for Racial Equality*. Trentham Books

Ouseley, H (2001) *Community Pride Not Prejudice: Making diversity work in Bradford*. Bradford Race Review

Owen, D (1992–95) *1991 Census Statistical Papers 1–9*. Centre for Research in Ethnic Relations, University of Warwick/CRE

Owen, D 'Size, structure and growth of the ethnic minority populations' *in* Coleman, D and Salt, J *eds* (1996) *Demographic characteristics of the ethnic minority populations, Ethnicity in the 1991 Census*. HMSO

Parekh, B (2000) *The Future of Multi-Ethnic Britain. The Parekh Report*. Runnymede Trust

Parker, R 'Counting with care; A re-analysis of the OPCS data' *in* Social Services Inspectorate and Council for Disabled Children (1998) *Disabled Children: Directions for their future care*. DoH

Pathak, S (2000) *Race Research for the Future: Ethnicity in education, training and the labour market*. DfEE

Payne, J (1969) A comparative study of the mental ability of 7 and 8 year old British and West Indian children in a West Midlands town, *British Journal of Educational Psychology*, 39, 326–7

Peach, C 'Introduction' *in* Peach, C *ed*. (1996) *Ethnicity in the 1991 Census Volume 2: The ethnic minority populations of Great Britain*. HMSO

Peoplescience Intelligence Unit (2000) *Black Child Report 1999–2000*. Peoplescience Intelligence Unit

Percy, A (1998) *Ethnicity and Victimisation: Findings from the 1996 British Crime Survey.* Home Office Statistical Bulletin

Press Complaints Commission (1999) *Code of Practice*

Prewett, B (2000) *Recruiting and Supporting Short-Break Carers for Children who are Considered 'hard to place'.* Joseph Rowntree Foundation

Prior, G, Courtenay, G and Charkin, E (1999) *2nd Survey of Parents of Three and Four Year Old Children and their use of Early Years Services.* Department for Education and Employment Research Brief 120

Pushkin, I (1967) *A Study of Ethnic Choice in the Play of Young Children in Three London Districts.* Unpublished Ph.D dissertation, University of London

Pushkin, I and Veness, T 'The development of racial awareness and prejudice in children', *in* Watson P ed. (1973) *Psychology and Race.* Penguin

Qualifications and Curriculum Authority (1999) *The Review of the National Curriculum in England, The consultation materials.* DfEE and QCA

Qualifications and Curriculum Authority (2000) *Curriculum Guidance for the Foundation Stage.* QCA

Qureshi, T, Berridge, D and Wenman, H (2000) *Where to Turn? Family support for South Asian Communities.* National Children's Bureau for the Joseph Rowntree Foundation

Race, T (1999) Hide and Seek, *Community Care 19–25 August*

Radke, M J, Trager, H G and Davis, H (1949) Social perceptions and attitudes of children, *Genetic Psychology*, 40, 327–447

Raleigh, V S and Balarajan, R (1995) The health of infants and children among ethnic minorities, *The Health of Our Children Dennial Suppl. 82–94.* The Stationery Office

Ramsay, M and Spiller, J (1997) *Drug Misuse declared in 1996: Latest results from the British Crime Survey.* Home Office.

Raynor, L (1970) *Adoption of Non-White Children: The Experiences of a British Adoption Project.* Allen and Unwin

Refugee Council (1997) *Helping Refugee Children in Schools.* Refugee Council

Rex, J (1970) *Race Relations in Sociological Theory.* Weidenfeld and Nicolson

Rex, J (1983) *Race Relations in Sociological Theory.* Routledge and Kegan Paul

Richards, A and Ince, L (2000) *Overcoming the Obstacles. Looked after Children: Quality Services for Black and Minority Ethnic Children and their Families.* Family Rights Group

Richards, G (1995) Supplementary Schools – their service to education, *Multicultural Teaching*, 14, 1, 36–40

Richardson, R and Wood, A (1999) *Inclusive Schools, Inclusive Society: Race and Identity on the Agenda.* Trentham Books

Robinson, C and Stalker, K (1993) Patterns of provision in respite care and the Children Act, *British Journal of Social Work*, 23, 1, 45–63

Rose, E J B, Deakin, N, Cohen, B and others (1969) *Colour and Citizenship.* Oxford University Press for the Institute of Race Relations

Rowe, J, Hundleby, M and Garnett, L (1989) *Child Care Now: A survey of placement patterns.* British Agencies for Adoption and Fostering

Runnymede Trust in partnership with the Commission for Racial Equality (1998) *Young People in the UK: Attitudes and Opinions on Europe, Europeans and the European Union.* The Runnymede Trust

Rutter, J (1995) *Refugee Children in British Schools.* Refugee Council

Rutter, M, Giller, H and Hagell, A (1998) *Antisocial Behaviour by Young People.* Cambridge University Press

Sammons, P, Sylva, K, Melhuish, E and others (1999) *Characteristics of the EPPE Project Sample at Entry to the Study. Technical paper no 2.* Institute of Education

Sarup, M (1986) *The Politics of Multicultural Education.* Routledge

Sarwar, G (1994) *British Muslims and Schools.* The Muslim Educational Trust

Scanlon, M, Earley, P and Evans, J (1999) *Improving The Effectiveness of School Governing Bodies.* DfEE

Scarman, Lord (1982) *The Scarman Report. The Brixton Disorders 10–12 April 1981.* Pelican Books

School of Oriental and African Studies (1997) *Language Survey.* SOAS

Sewell, T (1997) *Black Masculinities and Schooling, How black boys survive modern schooling.* Trentham Books

Shah, R (1995) *The Silent Minority: Children with disabilities in Asian families.* National Children's Bureau

Shah, R (1997) Improving services to Asian families and children with disabilities, *Child: Care, Health and Development,* 23, 141–6

Shah, R and Hatton C (1999) *Caring Alone: Young Carers in South Asian Communities.* Barnardo's

Shanahan, J (1995) Television viewing and adolescent authoritarianism, *Journal of Adolescence,* 18, 271–88

Sibbitt, R (1997) *The Perpetrators of Racial Harassment and Racial Violence.* Home Office

Singh, G (1992) *Race and Social Work: From 'Black Pathology' to 'Black Perspectives'.* Race Relations Research Unit

Singh, R K (2000) This is not an add-on. It's a must, *Quality Protects,* 6, 16

Siraj-Blatchford, I (1990) *The Experience of Black Students in Initial Teacher Education.* Department of Education

Sivanandan, A (1983) *A Different Hunger: Writings on black resistance.* Pluto Press

Skellington, R (1996) *'Race' in Britain Today.* Sage

Slater, M (1993) *Health For All Our Children: Achieving appropriate health care for black and minority ethnic children and their families.* Action for Sick Children, Quality Review Series

Smaje, C (1995) *Health, Race and Ethnicity. Making sense of the evidence.* Kings Fund Institute

Smith, P and Berridge, D (1993) *Ethnicity and Childcare Placements.* National Children's Bureau

Smith, P K and Sharp, S (1994) *School Bullying: Insights and perspectives.* Routledge

Smith, T (2000) A refuge for children? The impact of the Immigration and Asylum Act, *Poverty,* 105, 6–10

Social Exclusion Unit (1998) *Bringing Britain Together: A national strategy for neighbourhood renewal.* TSO

Social Exclusion Unit (1999) *Bridging the Gap: New Opportunities for 16–18 year olds not in Education, Employment or Training.* TSO

Social Services Inspectorate (1995) *The Challenge of Partnership in Child Protection: Practical guide.* HMSO

Social Services Inspectorate (2000a) *Excellence not Excuses: Inspection of services for ethnic minority children and families.* DoH

Social Services Inspectorate (2000b) *Modern Social Services: A commitment to people. The 9th annual report of the chief inspector of social services.* DoH

Soni Raleigh, V (1996) Suicide patterns and trends in people of Indian subcontinent and Caribbean origin in England and Wales, *Ethnicity and Health,* 1, 55–63

Soni Raleigh, V, Bulusu, L and Balarajan, R (1990) Suicides among immigrants from the Indian Subcontinent, *British Journal of Psychiatry,* 161, 365–8

Spencer, N (1996a) *Poverty and Child Health.* Radcliffe Medical Press

Spencer, N (1996b) Race and ethnicity as determinants of child health: A personal view, *Child Care, Health and Development,* 22, 5

Stern, G, Cottrell, D and Holmes, J (1990) Patterns of attendance of child psychiatry out-patients with special reference to Asian families, *British Journal of Psychiatry,* 156, 384–7

Stone, M (1981) *The Education of the Black Child in Britain: The myth of multiracial education.* Fontana

Storkey M (1994) *London's Ethnic Minorities: One city many communities.* London Research Centre

Storkey, M and Bardsley, M 'Estimating the numbers of refugees and asylum seekers in London' *in* Aldous, J and others *eds* (1999) *Refugee Health in London.* Health of Londoners Project

Strand, S (1999) Ethnic Group, Sex and Economic Disadvantage: Associations with pupils' educational progress from Baseline to the end of key stage 1, *British Educational Research Journal,* 25, 2

Stratford, N, Finch, S and Pethick, J (1997) *Survey of Parents of Three and Four Year Old Children and Their Use of Early Years Services.* DfEE

Streetly, A, Maxwell, K and Mejia, A (1997) *Sickle Cell Disorders in Greater London. A needs assessment of screening and care services. The fair shares for London report.* Department of Public Health Medicine, UMDS, St Thomas's Hospital

Sure Start (1999) *Guidance on Involving Minority Ethnic Children and Families.* DfEE

Swain, J and Eagle, P (1987a) The views of parents and carers: 1. some pleasures, stresses, and strategies, *Mental Handicap,* 15, 102–4

Swain, J and Eagle, P (1987b) The views of parents and carers, *Mental Handicap,* 15, 152–4

Swann Report (1985) *Education for All: Report of the Committee of Inquiry into the Education of Children from Ethnic Minority Groups.* Department for Education and Science

Teacher Training Agency (2000) *Raising the Attainment of Minority Ethnic Pupils: Guidance and Resource Materials for Initial Teacher Training Providers.* Final Draft

Teacher Training Agency (1999) *Initial Teacher Training Performance Profiles.* TTA

Thoburn, J, Lewis, A and Shemmings, D (1995) *Paternalism or Partnership? Family involvement in the child protection process.* HMSO

Thomas, A, Bax, M and Smyth, D (1988) The provision of support services for young adults with physical and mental handicaps, *Mental Handicap,* 16, 92–6

Thomas, L (1995) *Multi-cultural aspects of attachment.* Internet

Tizard, B (1977) *Adoption: A second chance.* Open Books

Tizard, B and Phoenix, A (1993) *Black, White or Mixed Race: Race and racism in the lives of young people of mixed parentage.* Routledge

Tovey, P, Atkin, K and Milewa, T (2001) The individual and primary care: service user, reflexive choice maker and collective actor, *Critical Public Health,* 11, 2, 2001

Troyna, B and Hatcher, R (1992) *Racism in Children's Lives.* Routledge/National Children's Bureau

United Kingdom Thalassaemia Society (undated) *Thalassaemia Fact Sheet*

United Nations General Assembly (1992) *The Declaration on the Rights of Persons belonging to National or Ethnic, Religious and Linguistic Minorities*

United Nations High Commissioner for Refugees (1994) *Refugee Children: Guidelines on Protection and Care*. UNHCR

Utting, W B (1990*) Issues of Race and Culture in the Family: Placement of Children*, Circular CI[90] 2, SSI, DoH

Utting, W (1997) People Like Us: The report of the review of the safeguards for children living away from home. DoH/Welsh Office

Warnes, T 'The Age Structure and Ageing of the Ethnic Groups' *in* Coleman D, and Salt, J *eds* (1996) *Ethnicity in the 1991 Census,* Vol 1. Office of Population Censuses and Surveys

Webb, W (1996) Meeting the needs of minority ethnic communities, *Archives of Disease in Childhood*. 74, 3 (Mar), 264–7

Wilson, A (1987) *Mixed Race Children: A study of identity.* Allen & Unwin

Wolke, D (1999) School anti-bullying tactics do not work, University of Herts. Quoted in *The Independent* and *The Times*, 14 December

Wolkind, S and Rutter, M 'Socio-cultural factors' *in* Rutter, M and Hersov, L *eds* (1985) *Child and Adolescent Psychiatry: Modern approaches* (2nd edition). Blackwell Scientific Publications

Woodbridge, J, Burgum, D and Heath, T (2000) *Asylum Statistics*. Home Office

Woods, P and Grudgeon, E 'Pupils, 'race' and education in primary schools' *in* Woodhead, M, Light, P and Carr, R *eds* (1991) *Growing Up in a Changing Society.* Routledge

Wright, C 'School Processes – an ethnographic study' *in* Eggleston, J, Dunn, D and Anjali, M (1986) *Education for Some: The educational & Vocational Experiences of 15–18 year old members of Minority Ethnic Groups.* Trentham

Wright, C (1992) *Race Relations in the Primary School.* David Fulton Publishers

Wright, C, Weekes, D and McGlaughlin, A (2000) *Race, Class and Gender in Exclusion from School*. Falmer Press

Yee, L and Au, S (1997) *Chinese Mental Health Issues in Britain: Perspectives from the Chinese Mental Health Association.* Mental Health Foundation

Youth Justice Board website: www.youth-justice-board.gov.uk

Yule, W, Berger, M, Rutter, M and Yule, B (1975) Children of West Indian immigrants: II. Intellectual performance and reading attainment, *Journal of Educational Psychiatry,* 16, 1–18

Author Index

Fryer, P 121

Gallagher, B 87
Gardner, C 129
Ghazala, A 78
Ghuman, P 16, ,18
Gibbons, J 87
Giddens, A 5
Gill, O 103
Gillborn, D 6, 43,44, 45, 46, 48, 49, 54, 56, 138, 140
Gipps, C 43, 48
Goodman, ME 8
Goodman, R 81
Gordon, P 128
Goulbourne, H 122
Graham, J 91
Grugeon, E 16

Hackett, L 81
Harland, J 17
Harris, P 126
Haslam, J 28, 65
Hatcher, R 140
Hatton, C 150
Henderson, P 24, 102
Hengst, H 129
Herbert, I 74
Hodes, M 82, 115

Ince, L 6, 99, 100, 107
Ivaldi, G 97

Jackson, B 103
Jacobson, B 83, 111, 114
Jadhav, S 82
Joly, D 110, 148
Jones, E 87
Julienne, L 142

Kahn, J 77
Kassam, N 159
Katz, I 8, 9, 159
Kaur, R 24, 102
Kinder, K 17, 47
Kohli, R 113
Kopraska, J 84
Kramer, T 81, 85

Laishley, J 7
Lane, J 6, 144, 145
Lau, A 15
Little, A 42

Little, J 64
Littlewood, R 82
Lomas, G 21

McCarraher, L 129
McCurdy, K 87
Macdonald, I 156
McDonald, J 116
MacDonald, S 134
McGibben, L 83
Macpherson, W 55, 95, 105, 122–3, 137, 139, 159
Madge, N 7, 11, 17, 87, 143
Malik, H 144
Martin, I 133
Mason, D 132
Merrill, J 82
Miles, J 97
Milner, D 7
Mirza, H 44, 45, 46, 56
Modood, T 10, 14, 18, 22, 25, 27, 28, 29, 31, 36, 128
Moffatt, PG 104
Moghal, NE 87
Morrison, M 55
Mukhtar, K 140
Mullix, M 71

Nadirshaw, Z 70
Nagra, JS 52
Neeleman, J 83
Nelson, F 151
Nicholl, A 64
Norton, R 114

Okitikpi, T 52
O'Neale, V 77, 84, 99, 100, 101, 107, 157
Osler, A 55
Ouseley, H 50, 125, 144, 159
Owen, D 23
Owen, M 88, 89, 106
Owens, J 82

Parekh, B 56, 60, 62, 63, 71, 150
Parker, R 75
Parton, N 88
Pathak, S 59, 61
Payne, J 42
Peach, C 4, 20, 23, 32
Phoenix, A 8, 12, 22, 142
Power, C 121
Prior, G 38
Pushkin, I 7

Subject Index